LADY AUDLEY'S SECRET:
A DRAMA IN TWO ACTS

LADY AUDLEY'S SECRET:
A DRAMA IN TWO ACTS

Mary Elizabeth Braddon and George Roberts

a *Broadview Anthology of British Literature* edition

Contributing Editor, *Lady Audley's Secret*:
Yevgeniya Traps, Barnard College

General Editors,
Broadview Anthology of British Literature:
Joseph Black, University of Massachusetts, Amherst
Leonard Conolly, Trent University
Kate Flint, Rutgers University
Isobel Grundy, University of Alberta
Don LePan, Broadview Press
Roy Liuzza, University of Tennessee
Jerome J. McGann, University of Virginia
Anne Lake Prescott, Barnard College
Barry V. Qualls, Rutgers University
Claire Waters, University of California, Davis

broadview press

Library and Archives Canada Cataloguing in Publication

Roberts, George, 1832-1912
    Lady Audley's secret : a drama in two acts / Mary Elizabeth Braddon and George Roberts ; contributing editor, Yevgeniya Traps ; general editors, Joseph Black ... [et al.].

(Broadview anthology of British literature)
ISBN 978-1-55481-160-1

    1. Braddon, M. E. (Mary Elizabeth), 1835-1915--Adaptations.
I. Black, Joseph, 1962- II. Traps, Yevgeniya, 1980- III. Title.
IV. Series: Broadview anthology of British literature

PR5232.R15L33 2013   822'.8   C2012-907268-0

Broadview Press is an independent, international publishing house, incorporated in 1985.

We welcome comments and suggestions regarding any aspect of our publications—please feel free to contact us at the addresses below or at broadview@broadviewpress.com.

North America	PO Box 1243, Peterborough, Ontario, Canada K9J 7H5
	2215 Kenmore Ave., Buffalo, New York, USA 14207
	Tel: (705) 743-8990; Fax: (705) 743-8353
	email: customerservice@broadviewpress.com
UK, Europe, Central Asia,	Eurospan Group, 3 Henrietta St., London WC2E 8LU, UK
Middle East, Africa, India,	Tel: 44 (0) 1767 604972; Fax: 44 (0) 1767 601640
and Southeast Asia	email: eurospan@turpin-distribution.com
Australia and New Zealand	NewSouth Books, c/o TL Distribution
	15-23 Helles Ave., Moorebank, NSW, Australia 2170
	Tel: (02) 8778 9999; Fax: (02) 8778 9944
	email: orders@tldistribution.com.au

www.broadviewpress.com

Developmental Editors: Jennifer McCue and Laura Buzzard

The editors would like to acknowledge the assistance of Natalie M. Houston, editor of the Broadview Edition of the novel *Lady Audley's Secret*, who was kind enough to advise on textual matters in the preparation of this edition.

Contents

Introduction

In many ways, the life of Mary Elizabeth Braddon—prolific writer, editor, and actress—was as sensational as the novel that made her name. The most famous work of an author who would come to be known as "Queen of the Circulating Library," *Lady Audley's Secret* was an extraordinary popular success in its own day, and has not been out of print since it first appeared in 1862. The novel established Braddon as a significant force in the world of mid-Victorian publishing, giving her much longed-for financial freedom and making her one of the most prominent women to earn a living through writing at the time. Together with Wilkie Collins, whose novel *The Woman in White* (1860) initiated the craze, Braddon came to embody the short-lived but intense phenomenon of the sensation novel, attracting untold readers with the shocking twists and turns of plots pitting bigamists, murderers, and arsonists against the accidental detectives who must uncover sordid secrets in order to save the day.

Born in London on 4 October 1835, Mary Elizabeth Braddon was the daughter of an Irish mother, Fanny White, and a Cornish father, Henry Braddon, a failed solicitor. When she was four, Braddon's parents separated, and her mother took Mary and her siblings to Sussex, where they remained until returning to London in 1843.

In 1857, contending with financial difficulties, her mother's fortune having expired, Braddon found work as an actress under the stage name "Mary Seyton." She had some success, appearing in several productions, but, in 1860, with support from an admirer, Braddon dedicated herself to writing full time. Her work was serialized in various publications, and, in 1861, her new novel *Lady Audley's Secret* began appearing in *Robin Goodfellow*, a literary journal published by John Maxwell. Although *Lady Audley's Secret* drew readers' attention, *Robin Goodfellow* ceased publication after thirteen issues; however, in response to popular demand, Maxwell found Braddon's work a new venue in another one of his periodicals, the *Sixpenny Review*. The novel was serialized in its entirety from January through December 1862, and appeared as a three-volume edition that same year. It was serialized again in the *London Journal* in 1863, a fact that might serve as evidence of the work's tremendous popularity.

The eponymous heroine of *Lady Audley's Secret* is a childlike woman of immense beauty who hides a terrible secret—one she is prepared to kill to keep concealed. The novel became the focus of critical outrage, with many reviewers warning of the perils of sensational plots. The controversy did not impede—and indeed perhaps fostered—the work's popularity, and *Lady Audley's Secret* was adapted for the stage by three different playwrights in 1863. The novel's echoes of the real-life case of Constance Kent, who had inspired a media frenzy in 1860 when she was accused of the murder of her four-year-old brother, further spurred the sensation it caused.

Braddon's next novel, *Aurora Floyd*, was serialized in *Temple Bar Magazine* from January 1862 to January 1863 and published as a three-volume edition in 1863; another work hinging on bigamy and murder, it cemented Braddon's role as foremost practitioner of the sensation genre. In the course of her career, she wrote more than eighty novels—many of which presented astute social criticism—as well as founding (1866) and editing (1866–76) *Belgravia*, an illustrated literary journal which serialized sensation fiction but also published essays on contemporary fashion, travel, and science. This remarkable productivity established Braddon as one of the most significant women in the world of Victorian publishing.

Her personal life was also eventful. After Braddon met the Irish publisher John Maxwell in 1860, she began living with him in 1861. The couple's relationship, which lasted until his death in 1895, was complicated by the fact that Maxwell's first wife was still very much alive, though confined to an asylum for the insane. The relationship was a subject of public controversy until this first wife died in 1874, enabling Braddon and Maxwell to marry. Braddon assumed a guardian role to Maxwell's five children, and she and Maxwell had six more children together. Two of Braddon's sons, W. B. Maxwell and Gerald Maxwell, also became novelists.

Braddon continued writing well into the Edwardian era, adapting her work to the changing demands of publishing, but despite her versatility, she remained firmly associated with the sensation novel. In 1913, Braddon attended the premier of the silent-film adaptation of *Aurora Floyd*. She died two years later, on 4 February 1915, at the age of seventy-nine.

Sensation Novels

In 1863, the venerable Victorian philosopher and critic H.L. Mansel (1820–71) published a scathing response to the sensation novel phenomenon in the *Quarterly Review*. He accused the genre of "preaching to the nerves instead of the judgment," neatly summarizing the sense that the sensation novel trafficked in the lowest of emotions and catered to the most depraved of appetites. Nonetheless, the vehemence of his disapproval might be understood as indication of the sensation novel's influence, its popular appeal, and its capacity to affect readers. Mansel's "Sensation Novels" thus captured the various implications of "sensation": the sensation novel made use of sensational topics in order to produce emotional and physical sensations in its readers and thus became a publishing sensation.

Sensation fiction had a ten-year heyday beginning in 1860, the year Wilkie Collins's novel *The Woman in White* concluded its serialization in the journal *All the Year Round*, edited by Charles Dickens. Despite this relatively short period of prominence and despite the generally outraged critical response, which had the effect of consigning the sensation novel to the realm of "low" culture, the genre had a marked influence on a number of established—and critically lauded—nineteenth- and twentieth-century authors. Henry James was an admirer, noting, in a essay in *Nation* (9 November 1865) that "[t]o [Wilkie] Collins belongs the credit of having introduced into fiction those mysterious of mysteries, the mysteries which are at our own doors," and T.S. Eliot famously celebrated Collins's 1868 novel *The Moonstone* as the first detective novel in English. No less an eminent Victorian than Charles Dickens incorporated sensational elements into his late novels, most notably *Great Expectations* (1861) and the unfinished *The Mystery of Edwin Drood* (1870), though Dickens expressed reservations about sensational representations of sexual licentiousness, as well as what he understood as an excessive allegiance to plot necessities, rather than character development.

The sensation novel had its roots in the Newgate novel, which dramatized the lives of infamous criminals, and in melodrama, particularly the staged Victorian melodramas, with their established character types put through the paces of scandalous plots; indeed, the designation "sensation novel" emerged from the correspondence of its representations to the "sensation scenes" presented on the Victorian stage. (That many sensation novels were, in turn, adapted for the stage suggests an interesting symmetry of influence.) The genre also had roots in the Gothic novels of the late eighteenth century, although sensation literature made an important change to Gothic conventions by relocating the illicit plot from the foreign climates of France and Italy to the realm of respectable, middle-class English domesticity. More notably—and more threateningly—the sensation novel suggested that the home was compromised by the woman at its center, transforming the paradigmatic image of the "angel in the house" into a fiend capable, as Lady Audley proves herself to be, of duplicity, bigamy, murder, and arson. It was this aspect of sensation, perhaps more than any other, that outraged Victorian critics. Writing in the 22 August 1863 issue of *The Living Age*, an anonymous reviewer opined:

> There is nothing more violently opposed to our moral sense, in all the contradictions to custom which they present to us, than the utter unrestraint in which the heroines of this order are allowed to expatiate and develop their impulsive, stormy, passionate characters. We believe it is one chief among their many dangers to youthful readers that they open out a picture of life free from all the perhaps irksome checks that confine their own existence…. The heroine of this class of novel is charming because she is undisciplined, and the victim of impulse; because she has never known restraint or has cast it aside, because in all these respects she is below the thoroughly trained and tried woman.

And, considering Lady Audley herself in an unsigned essay in *North British Review* (September 1865), W. Fraser Rae suggested that

> Lady Audley is at once the heroine and the monstrosity of the novel. In drawing her, the authoress may have intended to portray a female Mephistopheles; but, if so, she should have known that a woman cannot fill such a part. The nerves with which Lady Audley could meet unmoved the friend of the man she had murdered, are the nerves of a Lady Macbeth who is half unsexed, and not those of the timid, gentle, innocent creature

Lady Audley is represented as being.... All this is very exciting; but it is also very unnatural. The artistic faults of this novel are as grave as the ethical ones. Combined, they render it one of the most noxious books of modern times.

But more recent studies of the sensation novel have suggested that Lady Audley attracts attention precisely *because* of her depravity. Ann Cvetkovich writes in *Mixed Feelings: Feminism, Mass Culture, and Sensationalism* (1992), her study of the genre, that "[t]he sensation of repulsion produced by Lady Audley's criminality is indistinguishable from the fascination produced by her beauty; sensationalism consists in the indistinguishibility of the two feelings." That is, the sensation novel's willingness to expose and examine the secret, hidden currents and impulses of domestic life made it apparently irresistible to readers.

Lady Audley's Secret on the Stage

Further evidence of the sensation novel's popularity can be found in the frequency with which sensation novels were adapted for the theater. Even as respectable Victorian critics decried Lady Audley's unnatural crimes and criticized the female novelist who created her, audiences flocked to staged versions; three different theatrical adaptations of *Lady Audley's Secret* were performed in 1863. One such version was written by William E. Suter (1811–82), whom Braddon's publishers sued when he published the play. Another was the work of Colin Henry Hazelwood (1823–75), who frequently based his plays on popular novels; he also adapted Braddon's next novel, *Aurora Floyd*. The adaptation presented here, written by Robert Walters (1832–1912) under the pseudonym "George Roberts," was personally approved by Braddon. It was first performed at the Royal St. James Theatre on February 28, 1863, with the actress Louisa Ruth Herbert in the role of Lady Audley. The play, which heightened the melodramatic effects of the novel's sensational revelations, enjoyed a two-season run.

Even three theatrical versions were apparently not enough to appease the public appetite for all things *Lady Audley*: the novel was lovingly lampooned on 26 December 1863 during a Boxing Day performance of H.J. Byron's *1863; or, The Sensations of the Past Sea-*

son, which prominently featured a cross-dressing burlesque satire of Braddon's work. Byron's farcical presentation—as Lady Audley, the comic actor J.L. Toole bemoaned the lack of time in which to commit arson—simultaneously highlighted and delighted in making fun of the melodramatic elements of the sensation novel and the way these were necessarily dramatized on the stage.

If critics objected to sensation fiction's explicit treatment of transgressive subjects, they even more strongly condemned the effects such subjects had on the stage. Indeed, the sensation novel transported to the theater necessarily lost much of the subtlety that might be developed over the space of three volumes through condensation into two acts, which largely focused on the most sensational of plot points to the exclusion of other details. Henry Morley, writing in the 14 March 1863 issue of *The Theatrical and Musical Examiner*, opined that the play suffered from being "only in two acts." As such, Morley continued,

> the putting of the superfluous husband into the well follows so closely on the bigamy, the glow of the arson, again so closely on the stain of murder, and the interesting heroine goes mad so immediately, with the glow of the house she has burnt yet on her face, and the man she has burnt in it dying on a stretcher by her side, that the audience has a pudding all plum.

It bears noting that, in the Suter stage version, not only is the murder scene staged, but Lady Audley removes a poniard, a type of dagger, from her dress, "turns rapidly on Talboys and stabs him," causing him to "stagger[...] back against the wall of the well; the wall gives way with a crash, and he disappears, falling down into the well." Lady Audley promptly disposes of her weapon and "hurries off." Meanwhile, in Hazelwood's adaptation, Lady Audley strikes George Talboys with an iron handle from a well, exclaiming, "I am free! I am free! I am free! Ha, ha, ha!" But, subtle though they were not, theatrical presentations of sensation novels continued attracting audiences well into the twentieth century, when many were transformed into film versions.

Lady Audley's Secret: A Drama in Two Acts

Founded on, and in part adapted from, Miss Braddon's Novel of that Name, by George Roberts (Member of the Dramatic Authors' Society).

CHARACTERS

Sir Michael Audley
Robert Audley
George Talboys
Marks
Slip
First Countryman
Second Countryman
Servants

Lady Audley
Alice
Phoebe

Servants, Peasants, &c.

PERIOD—*Present Day.*

ACT I, Scene I

(Robert Audley's Chambers, Fig-Tree Court, Temple;[1] furnished in bachelor style; single-sticks, foils,[2] boxing gloves, and prints on the wall; cigar boxes, pipes, and books scattered about.)

(Slip busied arranging breakfast things—Robert Audley from inner room.)

AUDLEY. (*Without.*) Slip!

SLIP. Sir.

AUDLEY. Tea made?

SLIP. Yes, sir.

5 AUDLEY. Bacon broiled?

SLIP. Yes, sir.

AUDLEY. Egg done, two minutes and twenty seconds?

(Enter Robert Audley.)

SLIP. Yes, sir.

AUDLEY. Good! (*To Slip, going.*) Paper ironed?

10 SLIP. Boy hasn't been yet, sir.

AUDLEY. And you expect the digestive organ to get on without the assistance of the daily organ, eh, you young scamp? Off with you to the office!

SLIP. (*Going.*) Yes, sir. Oh! here's a letter, sir, that came by the

15 early post. (*Gives it and exit.*)

AUDLEY. (*Looking at address and reading it.*) "Robert Audley, Esq., Barrister-at-Law." This is my pretty cousin's handiwork. "Barrister-at-Law," with a note of admiration at one end, and a note of interrogation at the other. That's Alice's idea of a joke.

20 She's never happy unless she's pitching my profession into my teeth. It's too bad—too bad! If I can't command, at least I deserve success. For five years I have listened to the advice of

---

1 *Temple* Area of Central London and the location of two of the four Inns of Court, professional organizations for English and Welsh barristers.
2 *single-sticks, foils* Fencing equipment.

friends and foes. "Go to Westminster," says A, "and ventilate[1] yourself," so I would, if they'd ventilate the Courts. "Dine in hall," cries B; so I did at five: five o'clock for a whole term, till 25 I got dyspeptic.[2] "Stick to chambers," whispers a third, "and "wait for clients." Wait! Haven't I waited like Patience, on a hard cane chair, smiling at imaginary briefs? "Go circuit,"[3] bellows a fourth. Circuit! pshaw! haven't I been round and round and round again, like a squirrel in a cage, 'till I've lapsed into a state 30 of chronic vertigo? No; if I'd been a pauper like Plodder, or had married an attorney's only daughter, like Badger, or was a bum-bailiff's brother, like Bouncer, perhaps I might, by this time, have got one foot on the woolsack.[4] But, as it is, Blackstone has paled before Balzac;[5] and after all, I'm not much to be pitied. 35 What with a trip up the Rhine, or a peep at the Pyrenees, a day's cover-shooting, or a scour across country to shake up the liver, to say nothing of a stall at the Opera, and a cosy club, I manage to scratch through the year somehow. Then there's my uncle's honest face and cheery welcome at Audley Court, and— 40 Alice!—Alice! that reminds me of my letter. (*Opens it.*) Crossed and re-crossed, of course, and stuffed with the usual padding; abuse of Sir Michael's young wife, and mild banter about my legal deficiencies. Ah! What's this? "Papa expects you to come as soon as business will permit, and pay your homage to the wax 45 doll"—Wax doll!—that's my aunt—"who's dying to make your acquaintance." Poor Alice; there's clearly not room for two rival

---

1 *Westminster* Westminster Hall accommodated the Court of King's Bench, the Court of Common Pleas, and the Court of Chancery. In 1875, the three courts were unified as the High Court of Justice, which continued to meet at Westminster; *ventilate* Express an opinion.

2 *dyspeptic* Suffering from digestive difficulties, but also depressed.

3 *circuit* Route traveled by judges, lawyers, etc. through appointed areas for the purposes of holding court.

4 *bum-bailiff* Derisive term for an officer of the law, usually one charged with making arrests. According to Samuel Johnson's dictionary, "A bailiff of the meanest kind"; *on the woolsack* Reference to the office of the Lord Chancellor in the House of Lords. The origins of the term lie in the fact that the Lord Chancellor's seat was made of a large sack of wool.

5 *Blackstone* William Blackstone (1723–80), a noted English judge and conservative politician and the author of *Commentaries on the Laws of England*; *Balzac* Honoré de Balzac (1799–1850), French novelist and playwright.

queens at Audley Court. Dying to make my acquaintance, is she? Well, I'll gratify her, I'll go; for I am anxious, I own it, to
50 see the fair-haired Circe,[1] who has taken captive sober sixty-five. Yes, Slip shall pack up my traps[2] at once, and I'll run down this very afternoon. (*Knock heard at door.*) Halloa! What's that? A knock; it is too soft for a dun,[3] and too loud for—Ah! Slip, back with the *Times*, and forgot the key. I'll be bound; the careless
55 dog. (*Goes to door.*)

TALBOYS. (*Without.*) Is this Mr. Audley's?

AUDLEY. Yes, this is Mr. Audley's, my good man; and your business?

TALBOYS. (*Without.*) I'll tell you when I'm inside.

60 AUDLEY. But I don't know—

(*Enter Talboys, pushing Audley back.*)

TALBOYS. But I do. I know this much, that Bob Audley never yet sported the oak in Fig-Tree Court against his old Eton fag[4] and friend, George Talboys.

AUDLEY. George! (*Shaking hands.*)

65 TALBOYS. Ay, Bob, the same, though a little the worse for wear. I only touched British ground late last night, and came up by the morning express. As I was passing through town, I thought I'd sponge on you for a breakfast before—before I ran off to—to her.

70 AUDLEY. Her?

TALBOYS. Yes, my wife! But I forgot; you don't know my history, at least the history of the last three years.

AUDLEY. Why, man, how should I? I've neither seen nor heard of you since you caught the scarlet fever, and became a plunger.[5]

---

1 *Circe* Minor goddess in Greek mythology, occasionally called a witch or a nymph. In Homer's *Odyssey*, where she is described as "the loveliest of goddesses" (10.539 in Robert Fitzgerald's translation), Circe transforms Odysseus's men into swine, but after Odysseus spends a year as her lover, she offers her help in guiding his return to Ithaca.

2 *traps* Personal belongings; baggage.

3 *dun* Creditor or debt-collector.

4 *sported the oak* Shut the door; *fag* Junior student who serves, in English public schools like Eton, as a kind of gopher for a senior student.

5 *plunger* Soldier, a member of the cavalry.

But sit down, and let me get another cup and plate. The idea of   75
your having a wife, old boy! (*Goes up to cupboard.*)

TALBOYS.   No change there, time has dealt easier with him; just
the same laughing, listless fellow I left behind me.

AUDLEY.   (*Returning with cup and plate.*) Here we are; but stay.
First, by way of sharpening my appetite, you must tell me   80
all about your wife. So now "the truth, the whole truth, and
nothing but the truth."

TALBOYS.   My story is soon told, Bob—thanks to the purchase-
system and my father's assistance, I didn't rest a subaltern[1] long.
The monotonous routine of a cavalry regiment didn't bore   85
me much. At length we were moved to a rotten, worm-eaten
seaport, so dull and melancholy that to prevent falling into
mischief—

AUDLEY.   You fell in love—much the same thing.

TALBOYS.   I did. My pet lived with her father, a broken-down   90
half-pay lieutenant,[2] a drunken hypocrite, ready to sell his little
girl to the highest bidder. Do you think I didn't see through
his pastry-cook dinners and his public-house port, his shallow
tricks, and rusty traps—

AUDLEY.   Into which you tumbled, nevertheless.   95

TALBOYS.   I did, but with my eyes wide open. It was love at first
sight, and we made a match of it. My father was furious, and
illustrated his sentiments on the subject by stopping my yearly
allowance on—on our wedding day.

AUDLEY.   Then you sold out,[3] of course.   100

TALBOYS.   Yes, and the money I got for my commission kept us
afloat on the Continent for a few months. At last my darling
felt homesick, and coaxed me back under the roof of her old
drunken father, who proved his affection by draining the dregs
of our little stock.   105

AUDLEY.   Poor George!

---

1   *purchase-system* Practice of purchasing military commissions and army rank;
    subaltern Inferior.
2   *half-pay lieutenant* Retired officer receiving an allowance from the British Army or
    Royal Navy.
3   *sold out* Sold his army commission.

TALBOYS. I'm an easy-going fellow, as you know, Bob; but when the wolf *once* got to the door, I fairly gave way. One night Helen's tears and reproaches drove me mad. I flew into a rage

110 with her, her father, everybody, and left her, as I swore, for ever.

AUDLEY. And you kept your promise?

TALBOYS. No; for that same evening I stole back, when she was asleep, Bob, put a few pounds, the half of our small stock, on the table by the bed, kissed the pale baby-face, and crept like a

115 thief out of the room. Next night I was out at sea, bound for Melbourne, a steerage passenger, with a digger's[1] tools for my baggage, and a few shillings in my purse.

AUDLEY. And you succeeded?

TALBOYS. Not till I had long despaired of success. But I toiled on,

120 Bob; I toiled on steadily to the end, and in the end, I conquered.

AUDLEY. Bravo, Bravo! That's like the George of my old Eton days.

TALBOYS. No, no, 'twas through no courage of mine that I conquered: 'twas the memory of my darling, the trust I had in her love and truth that was the keystone of success; the one

125 star that lit up the thick black darkness of those weary times; through all the long and dreary day of that probation, her little white hand beckoned me onward to a happy future.

AUDLEY. But during all that time did you never write to her?

TALBOYS. Never; that is (*Hesitating.*)—n-not-not till a week

130 before we sailed. I hadn't the heart to write when all looked so black; I dared not tell her I was fighting with despair and death.

AUDLEY. (*Thoughtfully.*) And you have never heard from her?

TALBOYS. Not a line—not a word for three long years and more; but why? how should I? Why do you look so grave?

135 AUDLEY. Grave; was I? That's not a common case with me; I was only thinking, but—(*Changing his manner.*) but no matter.

TALBOYS. What! have I come back to find a Job's comforter[2] in Robert Audley? (*In a tone of alarm.*) Heavens, man, I read doubt, suspicion in your face. Why do you say—

---

1 *digger* Prospector.

2 *Job's comforter* One who magnifies suffering while pretending to relieve it. Cf. the Biblical Book of Job, which relates the story of Job's anguish at the destruction of his family and his friends' insistence that "Who, being innocent, has ever perished? Where were the upright ever destroyed?" (Job 4.7).

AUDLEY. Say, my good George; I—I say nothing.   140

TALBOYS. Why do you torture me, when I'm going home to the
woman I love?—to her whose heart is fixed as the light above,
and in whom I no more expect to find a change than I do to see
a second sun rise in to-morrow's sky. Why put idle fancies into
my head when I'm going to her?   145

AUDLEY. My dear George, you are excited, and under the
circumstances, I'm not surprised you should be. Now I think of
it, if you didn't write, it is but natural you shouldn't have heard
from her.

TALBOYS. I have written to her father's house, given her the name   150
of my vessel, and the date of my probable arrival, and put "to be
forwarded" upon the letter. What more would you have?

AUDLEY. Then there can be no mistake.

TALBOYS. The *Argus* only got into port late last night. I couldn't
wait to see my luggage pass the Customs, but came up at once,   155
and here I am, and in a minute shall be off again to my own
true, my darling wife.

AUDLEY. And I only wish I could be with you to share the pleasure
of the meeting, George; but come; breakfast, breakfast.

TALBOYS. You shall see her before many days, Bob, I've built all   160
sorts of airy castles during the voyage. I think of taking a villa
on the Thames, Bob, and we'll have a yacht, old fellow, and the
little woman shall sing, and you shall lie on the deck and smoke
your pipe and read French novels;[1] but I suppose you've done
with that style of literature now?   165

AUDLEY. Not a bit of it.

TALBOYS. But doesn't it interfere with—with your practice, Bob?

AUDLEY. Practice! Ha, ha, ha! I didn't give you credit for being
such a wag,[2] George.

TALBOYS. Why, what do you mean? Have you given up the bar?   170

---

1   *French novels* French novels were often perceived by English critics as scandalous in
their depiction of relatively explicit sexual themes and transgressive relationships. Like
sensation fiction, they were believed to take advantage of the reader's reaction, and fears
were sounded about their addictive qualities, as well as their potential effects on the
reader's body. Furthermore, as an idle pastime, novel reading was coded as feminine in
Victorian England.

2   *wag* Joker.

AUDLEY. Given it up —not I; it never let me have the chance. It has given me up long ago. Themis[1] distributes her favours very sparingly, I can tell you. You may scrape a little gold dust by perseverance; but the Westminster diggings don't treat us all to
175   a monster nugget.

TALBOYS. Well, you've no cause to complain. You're not poor, and you've a rich uncle.

AUDLEY. Ay, and as good as he is generous, with as kind a heart as ever beat; but we're none of us fire-proof, George; and Cupid's
180   torch has set poor Sir Michael alight like so much tinder.

TALBOYS. What, married again?

AUDLEY. Yes, fallen into the same trap as yourself; bound hand and foot by silken chains and golden locks. Half Essex is raving about the new mistress of Audley Court. In short, my aunt is
185   the last county sensation.

TALBOYS. And how does she agree with you?

AUDLEY. Oh, admirably! We've never met yet, but I thought of running down this very afternoon.

TALBOYS. Ah, but you've another attraction, if I remember right,
190   at Audley Court, Master Bob; there's a certain cousin, isn't there?

AUDLEY. Certain—uncertain you mean. George, in my dreaming hours I've built my castles and villas on the Thames. Villas (*Lighting cigar.*) begot and ended in smoke.

TALBOYS. Come, come, don't despair; you're destined for
195   something better than drifting away under the care of a laundress in musty chambers; not but that you're very snug and comfortable here.

AUDLEY. Yes, I am comfortable, that's it.

TALBOYS. But you'd be a great deal more comfortable if that
200   certain uncertain little party would condescend to take you in hand. She'd effect a wonderful reformation.

AUDLEY. Revolution you mean; what would become of the pipes and the single-sticks?

TALBOYS. The boxing gloves and the *Pets of the Parterre*.[2] (*Pointing to prints.*)

---

1   *Themis* In Greek mythology, the goddess of law and justice.
2   *Pets of the Parterre* Subtitled "Or Love in a Garden: A Romantic Comedietta," this one-act play by J. Stirling Coyne was published c. 1860.

AUDLEY. And Balzac, Dumas and Son?[1] There'd be a regular   205
clearance wouldn't there? An alarming sacrifice?

TALBOYS. Owing to extensive alterations in business, that's it, Bob.
You'd get business, I know you would, married men always do.

AUDLEY. Yes, you're right, they do. I don't know why, unless it is
because they've a *double* claim.   210

TALBOYS. Ay, and you'd make a hit, take my word for it.

AUDLEY. That would depend on the subject. I have a twist for a
nice will case, with all sorts of contradictory clauses; or what
would be more to my taste, a good murder—a murder, George,
that would do a fellow credit, a tortuous devious plot, clogged   215
with subtle points of evidence, and encumbered with mystery;
a case that would take months, not minutes, to master. Gad,
George, give me that chance, and my fortune's made.

TALBOYS. Ha, ha, ha! to think of you being such a bloodsucker,
Bob; why you're a regular vampire in—in horsehair.[2]   220

AUDLEY. I've got it in me, George, but I've never had the luck to
bring it out, but perhaps the time may come.

TALBOYS. And for your sake, old boy, the sooner the better. I'm
afraid I can't get up a murder for you, but I think I'd go as far as
a trespass or a breach of the peace, to oblige an old friend.   225

AUDLEY. Thank you, I'll take the will for the deed; but this legal
rejoindering makes one thirsty. (*Producing tankard.*[3]) You
haven't forgotten Bass and Allsop at Burra-Burra?[4] (*Pouring
beer.*)

TALBOYS. Forgotten! I should think not. I had good reasons to
remember them. Why, this would stand you in a dollar at the   230
Antipodes.[5]

---

1 *Dumas and Son* Alexandre Dumas, *père* (1802–70), French novelist, best known
for his historical romances such as *The Three Musketeers*, and Alexandre Dumas, *fils*
(1824–95), his son and author of *The Lady of the Camellias*.

2 *in horsehair* English barristers typically wear horsehair wigs when appearing before a
judge.

3 *tankard* Drinking mug, typically used for beer.

4 *Bass and Allsop* The Bass Brewery, founded in 1777, and Samuel Allsop and Company,
founded in the 1740s, were the two largest breweries in England; *Burra-Burra* The
Burra Burra Copper Mine was established in the South Australian town of Burra in
1848, attracting an influx of prospectors and fortune hunters.

5 *Antipodes* Places understood to be direct opposites on the globe's surface. Thus, here a
reference to Australia.

AUDLEY. By Jove! you don't say so? Then I'll refuse the Chief Justiceship of Botany Bay,[1] when—when I get it.

(*Enter Slip, with* Times.)

(*To Slip.*) Back at last, you young rogue?

235 SLIP. The first issue was gone, sir, and there was an awful run on the second edition. (*Exit.*)

AUDLEY. (*Taking paper and reading.*) Let us see what's the news, "Copper moping, mule twist declining, pig iron dull, and grey shirtings[2] lively." That's interesting. (*Tossing paper to Talboys.*)

240 I suppose you haven't seen Sir Oracle[3] for many a long day, George?

TALBOYS. No; a paper from the old country is a rare treat for us in the far West. We don't send it to the butterman.[4]

AUDLEY. A back number has been my friend through many a

245 weary hour. I go the whole hog, and devour everything from the advertisements to—

TALBOYS. (*Reading.*) "The old maid's corner."

AUDLEY. Yes, from Alpha to Omega; so three cheers with all my heart for the Fourth Estate[5]—(*Drinks, as he puts down tankard*

250 *he notices Talboys, who is staring wildly at the paper.*)—Eh, why, what have you got hold of? Is Jupiter too much for you? (*Talboys makes no reply.*) Heavens, man, what's the matter?

TALBOYS. (*In a hollow tone pointing to paper.*) There, there!

AUDLEY. (*Taking paper and slowly reading as Talboys buries his face*

255 *in agony.*) "Died on the 20th inst.,[6] at Ventnor, Isle of Wight, Helen Talboys, aged 21."

---

1   *Botany Bay* Bay in Sydney, the site of the first English settlement in Australia.

2   *mule twist* Cotton yarn manufactured on a spinning mule, a factory spinning machine; *shirtings* Material used for manufacturing shirts. Throughout, Robert Audley is consulting the performance of various stocks.

3   *Sir Oracle* Cf. *The Merchant of Venice*: "As who should say, *I am Sir Oracle, / And when I ope my lips, let no dog bark!*" (1.1).

4   *send it … butterman* I.e., discard it as waste paper.

5   *Fourth Estate* The press.

6   *inst.* Of the current month.

ACT I, Scene 2

(A part of the Grounds at Audley Court.)

(Marks enters trimming stake with knife.)

MARKS. Under-keeper[1] at Audley Court! You ain't got much of
a lift, I'm thinking, Luke Marks. Under-keeper! I hate being
under anybody. I'd like to be independent. If it warn't for the
pickins to be got out of the old squire's preserves, I'd a' been off
long ago. Ha! ha! A net in the meadow and a wire in the wood,   5
a springe in the spinney,[2] and a night line in the pond;—that's
what I call bein' your own preserver. Well, where's the harm?
Self-preservation is the first law (that is, the first game law) of
natur', and I'm very much obliged to natur' for bringing it into
Parliament. Then there's Phoebe here—I can't go without her;   10
not that I often clap eyes on the gal, now that my lady has taken
her into her service. To be sure, my lady gives her double wages,
and odds and scraps o' left off finery she's too proud to wear; but
if I were in Phoebe's place, I'd feather my nest with something
better than ribbon and muslin. Only to hear Phoebe talk o' my   15
lady's jewels and treasures, why one o' them shinin' things she
showed me t'other day, would set a man up in life.

(Enter Phoebe over stile, softly and unnoticed by Marks.)

PHOEBE. *(On stile, putting her hand on his shoulder.)* What, Luke?
MARKS. *(Starting.)* Holloa! Why Phoebe, you give me the shivers
comin' down so still and sudden. I took you for a ghost.   20
PHOEBE. *(Laughing.)* A ghost? Well, I meant to surprise you. I
saw you from the window yonder, and thought I'd come down
and have a chat. Are you glad to see me, Luke?
MARKS. Glad? why of course I'm glad; why do you ask?
PHOEBE. Because you don't seem so; if you are, you might look   25
at me, and tell me if you think the journey has improved me.

---

1 *Under-keeper* Secondary custodian.
2 *springe* Small trap, typically used to catch birds; *spinney* Shrubbery.

MARKS. It ain't put any fresh colour in your cheeks, Phoebe. You used to be as plump as a pippin, and as brown as a russet,[1] and now you're as white as if you really were a ghost.

30 PHOEBE. But it's not genteel to have a colour, so my lady says.

MARKS. Genteel! Who wants you to be genteel? Not I for one; don't think it.

PHOEBE. But all the world isn't of your opinion, Luke. I'd lots o' pleasant things said to me when we were travelling; the couriers

35 and the valets paid me such compliments.

MARKS. That's like their sauce. *Curriers* indeed! I'd *curry*[2] 'em and no mistake.

PHOEBE. Why, you ought to be proud of people noticing me. Do you know, Luke, I learned more in the last three months abroad,

40 than I did in a year's schooling. And what do you think, Luke? I can speak a little French, and I've got as far as the irregular verbs.

MARKS. French! A deal o' use that'll be to you when you're Mrs. Marks; you won't have much time for any verbs, young woman,

45 *reglar* or not. French indeed! what next? Why, I suppose instead of your milk-pail, you'll go out with your grammar and begin *parley-vooing* to the cows.

PHOEBE. Come, come, Luke, don't be cross; it isn't my fault if my lady takes a fancy to me.

50 MARKS. She won't take a fancy to me, I'll take my oath o' that; not that I care a ha'porth[3] for her pride—she ain't no better than other folks.

PHOEBE. But she's richer and happier too, Luke; it's a fine thing, after all, to travel about in a chariot and four,[4] with a husband

55 by your side as thinks nothing's good enough for you, isn't it?

MARKS. It's a fine thing, Phoebe, to have lots o' money; but what was she, I'd like to know, a few months back, what but a servant like you and me—a governess at old Dawson's, the 'pothecary's,[5] taking wages and working for 'em too.

---

1   *pippin* Seed of a fruit; *russet* Type of potato with reddish-brownish peel.
2   *curry* Beat.
3   *ha'porth* Half a penny's worth.
4   *chariot and four* Light carriage pulled by four horses.
5   *'pothecary* Apothecary; a pharmacist.

PHOEBE. Yes! and her clothes so mean and shabby; and look at   60
  her now, Luke, as fine—
MARKS. As fine as the lady we saw at the show in the fair, all
  spangles and satin. Ay! she's a lucky one.
PHOEBE. With a crowd of fashionable gentlemen hanging around
  her, and she lighting up the old dull place with her sunny smiles   65
  and golden hair. Look at Lucy Graham now, the mistress of
  Audley Court, and the talk of the whole country.
MARKS. Well, well, never mind her, take care of yourself, Phoebe,
  that's your look out, and make hay while the sun shines. What
  should you say now to a public-house[1] for you and me? There's   70
  something to my mind independent in a public-house.
PHOEBE. But it's such noisy work, Luke.
MARKS. Pooh! it's cheerful, that's all. Don't ye be afraid, gal,
  I'll keep order, (*Flourishing stick.*) I'll do the knock-'em-down
  business while you serve 'em out wi' the pick-me-ups. With a   75
  bit o' cherry ribbon in your cap, you wouldn't look so dusty
  behind the bar.
PHOEBE. Yes! but think o' the money we should want.
MARKS. There's the "Chequers," at Mount Stanning, in the
  market; if you spoke to my lady, Sir Michael would put us up,   80
  I know.
PHOEBE. Ay! *she* can do anything with *him*.
MARKS. And *you* can do anything with *her*.
PHOEBE. What do you mean, Luke?
MARKS. I've heard you say as much. One o'them brilliants,[2]   85
  Phoebe, would buy the "Chequers" and to spare.
PHOEBE. Hush, Luke, how can you talk so?
MARKS. Have you got one o' them about you, gal, eh? (*Seizing
  her.*)
PHOEBE. Don't, Luke, let me go; I did very wrong to let you see   90
  that bracelet; I shouldn't, if you hadn't teased me.
MARKS. You promised to show me the house, and the fine gildings
  and looking glasses, and my lady's room. Are there more jewels
  there, Phoebe?

---

1 *public-house* Pub.
2 *brilliants* Finely cut diamonds.

95   PHOEBE. More! why there's a box crammed with rubies and diamonds, and emeralds and pearls; pearls, Luke, as big as—as pigeons' eggs.

MARKS. As pigeons' egg, eh? Egad! I'd like to take 'em to the pop-shop[1] in Chelmsford and hatch them, Phoebe—hatch 'em into
100 a brood of golden guineas.

PHOEBE. That's it—you're always wanting to be rich of a sudden, like the young man in the fairy tale. If we are to get married, Luke, we must work—work hard.

MARKS. Work hard! Well, so I do. What do you think o' that
105 (*Pulling gin from pocket.*) as a specimen of hard work? Short and sweet for the rabbits in the warren.[2]

PHOEBE. Poaching, Luke, still?

MARKS. Pooh! Poaching! No, I'm only looking after my perquisites.[3] But I say, Phoebe, about them pigeons' eggs, I'd
110 like to see 'em. Can't you take me round now, Phoebe?

PHOEBE. No, not now, Luke? My lady is in. They're expecting company. Mr. Robert is coming down to-morrow.

MARKS. What! the young counsellor? Him as is licensed to shoot the hen-pheasants? He's a regular tailor,[4] too, after the hounds;
115 I heard Sir Harry Towers say so.

PHOEBE. Of course he'd say so—he hasn't a chance of Miss Alice when Mr. Robert is here; he has quite turned her head.

MARKS. That's about all he can turn, for he's a poor hand at his trade; Lawyer Pounce told me he'd never earn his sake by—Eh!
120 (*Picks up bag.*) What's this?

PHOEBE. Why, if it isn't my lady's bag; she was sketching here this morning. Give it to me, Luke.

MARKS. There's no harm in having a peep.

PHOEBE. No, no. (*Trying to take it.*)

125 MARKS. (*looking in bag.*) Hum! only a handkerchief and a card case. Eh! what's this, Phoebe? See here, this bump in the leather; there's a inside pocket.

---

1   *pop-shop* Pawnshop.
2   *warren* Plot of land intended for rabbit breeding; network of rabbit burrows.
3   *perquisites* Non-inherited properties.
4   *tailor* Term of disparagement.

PHOEBE. Don't, Luke; give it me, (*Taking bag.*) your hands will
mark it. Ah! something in paper. (*Taking it out.*)

MARKS. May be one o' them pigeon's eggs. (*As Phoebe opens*   130
pocket.) Ugh! a wisp o' hair, and—a baby's shoe.

PHOEBE. You bear me witness where I found this, Luke. (*Puts
parcel in pocket.*)

MARKS. Why, you're never going to keep that rubbish? You are a
fool, Phoebe.   135

PHOEBE. Perhaps I am. I tell you what, Luke, I'd rather have these
than all the jewels in my lady's box.

MARKS. What do you mean?

PHOEBE. (*Going.*) I'll tell you some other time.

MARKS. What maggot is in your brain, gal? What are you   140
thinking of?

PHOEBE. Thinking? (*With emphasis.*) I was thinking, Luke, you'd
get the "Chequers" at Mount Stanning, that was all.

(*Exit over stile.*)

MARKS. Close! close as a hare in her form; so, so, have it your own
way now, Miss Phoebe; but when we start for the matrimonial   145
stakes, hang me, if the grey mare shall be the better horse.[1]

(*Exit.*)

---

1   *the grey ... better horse* Proverbial expression for a wife who dominates her husband.

ACT I, SCENE 3

(Library at Audley Court; at c.,[1] large bay window opening into garden; view of Well at back; picture covered with cloth on chair.)

(Lady Audley discovered at work,[2] Alice reading.)

LADY A. Alice?

ALICE. Yes, Lady Audley. (*Closing the book.*)

LADY A. *Lady* Audley! Your formality freezes me. Why not Lucy?

ALICE. I don't know; it seems more natural to—

5 LADY A. Reject my affection when I offer it? Come, come, Alice, why shouldn't we follow the laws of chemical affinity, and like Mr. Dawson's acids and alkalis, harmoniously combine.

ALICE. *Acids* and *alkalis*! you mean that I am—

LADY A. Whichever you please, my dear. But after all, why should
10 we quarrel? You look upon me as an intruder; I'm sorry for it. In marrying Sir Michael, I never contemplated robbing you of your father's love.

ALICE. You *could* not, if you would. (*Engaged with book.*)

LADY A. Of course not; all I have to ask of you in return is not
15 to injure me.

ALICE. Injure you! Lady Audley, how should *I* injure you?

LADY A. By seeking to deprive me of his affection.

ALICE. It would be idle to attempt so much. Your own act alone could wrest that from you.

20 LADY A. Now Alice, Alice, that is a roundabout way of saying I am deceitful. I am quite aware I am no better than other people, but it is not my fault if I am pleasanter, Alice. It's— it's—constitutional. (*Pause.*) Well, I must use my influence with your cousin, and try and get him to reconcile us.

25 ALICE. I have no doubt Mr. Robert Audley will be quite ready to listen to any arguments of yours.

LADY A. I hope he will. Do you know, Alice, I am dying to see him; something whispers we shall be fast friends.

---

1 *c.* Center stage.
2 *work* Needlework.

ALICE. Very likely. Robert Audley is too idle to make many enemies.   30

LADY A. Ah! then we will do our best to encourage his lazy habits; he shall have a hammock in the Lime Walk, and doze over his novels all day long. He is quite a curiosity, isn't he ?

ALICE. In being curious about nothing, yes; he doesn't attempt to make himself useful.   35

LADY A. No matter as long as he doesn't make himself *disagreeable*, but (*Looking off.*) here comes Sir Michael, and somebody with him too.

ALICE. (*Going to window.*) Robert. I declare! Now that's just like him, when he wasn't expected till to-morrow, pouncing upon,   40
and taking us by surprise. (*Looking out of window.*)

LADY A. And quite right too; for my part I like being taken by surprise.

ALICE. (*Aside.*) Now to scold him, and make myself thoroughly objectionable.   45

LADY A. (*Aside.*) And now for a first impression. It would be but poor policy to make a foe of Sir Michael's favourite.

(*Enter Sir Michael with Robert Audley.*)

SIR M. In with you, Bob, shyness we know is not your *forte*. (*To Lady A.*) Lucy, my love, let me introduce you to the *poacher* I encountered in the hazel copse;[1] he is unarmed.   50

AUDLEY. (*Aside.*) But she is fully prepared, and with the fatal panoply of Venus. (*Bowing.*)

SIR M. My nephew, Robert Audley, Lucy, barrister, of the Southern Circuit—full of brains, but short of briefs, eh, Bob?

LADY A. (*Extending her hand.*) And panting, I have no doubt,   55
for an opportunity of setting the woolsack on fire. When I am attacked, Mr. Audley, I shall retain you as my champion.

AUDLEY. In that case my chance of a brief is, I fear, hopeless. (*Aside.*) The idea of that fairy creature being my aunt, it's preposterous. (*To Alice.*) Not a word for me, cousin?   60

---

1   *copse* Tree grove.

ALICE. Not a good one, for you don't deserve it. (*Aside to Audley.*) Why are you not on your knees, before the wax idol?

AUDLEY. (*To Alice.*) So I would, only I'm afraid of melting her.

ALICE. Or rather of being melted.

65 AUDLEY. Why what a jealous little goose you are, Alice!

LADY A. And now that Mr. Audley—

SIR M. Mr. Audley? no, no, Mr. Bob, if you please; he's always Bob here.

LADY A. Well, then, Mr. Bob, tell me where shall you be most 70 at home, with your pipes and cigars, and least regretful of the Sybarite[1] luxury of Fig-Tree Court? Shall it be the blue room or the oriel,[2] or—

SIR M. Neither, my love. What do you think, this eccentric fellow will insist in putting up at the village inn (*Alice looking* 75 *enquiringly.*) because—

AUDLEY. Exactly, *because*, there's reason in everything. Lady Audley, because I can't persuade my dear old friend, George Talboys (*Lady Audley starts suddenly, but recovers herself immediately.*) to share your hospitality with me. (*To Alice.*) It 80 was owing to him I was prevented coming down a month ago. (*To Lady Audley.*) It's a sad story.

LADY A. Then pray don't let us hear it.

AUDLEY. It's useless trying to persuade him. Ever since his wife's death—

85 LADY A. Oh! don't apologise, pray; we can all appreciate your kind feeling. Your first duty is to your friend (*To Sir Michael.*) Is it not?

SIR M. Ye—yes, I suppose he must have his own way; Bob is as obstinate as a mule.

90 AUDLEY. I can't desert George Talboys; if you knew, uncle, what the poor fellow has suffered—

LADY A. Now don't tell us, please, don't tell us; I should dream of it. (*To Sir Michael.*) Shouldn't I, dear?

---

1 *Sybarite* Sensual, hedonist; dedicated to sensory gratification.

2 *oriel* Large space shaped like a polygon, typically located on the upper floor of a house.

Sɪʀ M. You mustn't frighten my little dove. But Bob, old boy, after your hot walk, what do you say to a glass of sherry, or some cyder cup? 95

Lᴀᴅʏ A. Yes, *do* have some cyder cup, Robert.

Sɪʀ M. And Alice shall immortalise the brew with a sprig of burrage.[1]

Aᴜᴅʟᴇʏ. Culled by her own fair hands— 100

(*Exit Sir Michael.*)

Aʟɪᴄᴇ. It's a great deal more than you deserve, tantalizing me in this way.

Lᴀᴅʏ A. And you really won't stay to dinner?

Aᴜᴅʟᴇʏ. Impossible, George—

Lᴀᴅʏ A. (*Quickly.*) But when your friend can spare you? 105

Aᴜᴅʟᴇʏ. I shall be ready to do your bidding. *Au revoir*, my dear aunt. Come, Alice. (*Aside.*) Hang me, if I'm not beginning to wish myself in my uncle's gouty slippers.

(*Exit Alice, followed by Robert.*)

Lᴀᴅʏ A. (*Alone.*) He lives! George Talboys lives! more, he is here in the village, not a mile from hence! Is then the present but a 110 dream, and is he come to drag me back into the hideous past? What shall I do? 'Tis he—yes, he, who has forced this load of guilt upon me! Why is he here? To taunt me with the memory of that night—that night which changed all—that night which smiled upon an artless trusting girl—that night whose 115 morrow's sun scowled with a brazen frown on the deserted wife and woke up, to another life a—a woman! While he is in the neighbourhood I am bound hand and foot, and cannot move for fear of exposure. There is no passion betwixt love and hate, and if we meet—but no; that cannot, must not be—(*Rings bell.*) 120 it is too late now. With your own hand, George Talboys, you have made your bed of shame and sorrow, and you shall lie upon it!

---

1   *burrage* Borage, herb used in the preparation of mixed drinks such as cider cup.

(*Enter Phoebe.*)

Phoebe, come here, child!

125 PHOEBE. How pale you look my, lady; are you ill?

LADY A. No; I feel a little tired, nothing more. Phoebe, have my trunks packed and all in readiness, I may go to London to-morrow, early.

PHOEBE. But the party at the Abbey and the ball, my lady?

130 LADY A. Do as I bid you.

PHOEBE. But Sir Michael, my lady, does he know?

LADY A. Don't pester me with questions, child! (*Going to desk and taking letter, which she gives Phoebe.*) After dinner bring me this letter, as if it had come by the late post, do you understand?

135 PHOEBE. Yes, my lady; but—

LADY A. Phoebe! I have trusted you, see that you do not abuse that confidence. You know enough, girl—too much already. Now go!

PHOEBE. Only one moment. I want to speak to your ladyship
140 about Marks, Luke Marks.

LADY A. What of him?

PHOEBE. He—he found this bag to-day. (*Gives bag to Lady Audley.*)

LADY A. (*Looking sternly at her.*) Phoebe, you have told that man!

145 PHOEBE. I couldn't help it; he forced it from me. Luke wants to marry me, my lady.

LADY A. (*Aside.*) In his power, too. (*Aloud.*) And *you* are in love *with him.*

PHOEBE. I don't think I can love him, but I promised years ago to
150 be his wife. I don't think I can break that promise now.

LADY A. And I say you shall *not* marry him. In the first place, I hate him; in the next, I cannot afford to part with you.

PHOEBE. My good, kind mistress, you don't know Luke Marks. 'Twill be my ruin if I break my word. I *must* marry him.

155 LADY A. But he has nothing, and how do you mean to live?

PHOEBE. That's what I was going to speak to you about, my lady. Luke wants to get the "Chequers" at Mount Stanning, and if you would say a word to Sir Michael—

LADY A. I see, I see; he *must* have the public-house, and the sooner he drinks himself to death the better for you and everybody. Ah! here comes Sir Michael, I'll speak to him at once. (*To Phoebe, going.*) Remember, have all prepared. 160

PHOEBE. I'll not forget; you are very good, my lady.

LADY A. Don't thank me. (*Exit Phoebe.*) (*Alone.*) I can't afford to refuse her. (*To Sir Michael, who re-enters.*) Well, my love, I hope you have been attentive to our nephew. His natural, easy manner is quite refreshing; he is far too frank and open for a lawyer. 165

SIR M. Bob is a capital fellow, Lucy; I was sure you'd like I him. It is a pity he can't induce his friend to take up his quarters with us. 170

LADY A. Oh, poor man, just lost his wife; widowers, you, know, dear, are sad bores.

SIR M. A left-handed compliment[1] for somebody, eh, Lucy?

LADY A. I mean till they are recaptured. "A burnt child,"[2] you know. It isn't everybody who has your courage, dear. 175

SIR M. Nor every woman of twenty, Lucy, the good nature to take pity on an old sexagenarian.

LADY A. Then you don't repent your bargain. But come, Sir Michael, I have a favour to ask you on Phoebe's part—(*In a coaxing tone.*) I am going to be *very* importunate. Let us talk it over in the other room, and leave a fair field here for the pair of pigeons yonder, Alice and Mr. Aud—I mean Mr. Bob. (*Sir Michael and Lady Audley go off.*) 180

(*Enter Alice and Robert Audley from the opposite side.*)

ALICE. And so the tap-room of the village inn has more charms for you than the society of Audley Court? 185

AUDLEY. How silly you are, Alice. Haven't I told you George would be ill at ease here. No, we must do the best for a few days; I dare say the cigar-boxes will be empty, and the fishing-tackle broken by the end of the week.

---

1 *left-handed compliment* Backhanded compliment; disparagement disguised as praise.
2 *"A burnt child"* Cf. the proverbial expression, "A burnt child dreads the fire."

190 ALICE. And Captain Talboys will lose the chance of seeing *"the most charming woman in Essex."* You know you said so, Robert.

AUDLEY. How you make a poor devil eat his words: you—you'd provoke a saint, Alice.

ALICE. Little fear then of provoking *you.*

195 AUDLEY. That's it, don't spare me. She is charming, you can't deny it; but she'd stand a poor chance of getting much admiration out of George. Poor fellow, his heart is in his wife's grave in Ventnor churchyard.

ALICE. Well, I suppose we must appreciate Damon's attention to 200 Pythias.[1] Ah, the dressing bell! (*Going.*) Don't forget, you must not run away without introducing me to your romantic friend.

AUDLEY. I'll entice him over some day—(*As Alice looks out of window.*) Eh, what's the matter?

ALICE. (*Pointing.*) Look! a stranger in the Lime Walk.

205 AUDLEY. (*At window, looking out.*) Why, if it isn't George in *propria persona.*[2] Lost all patience, I suppose, or lost his way. I'll have him in, if only to gratify your curiosity. (*Runs out.*)

ALICE. Poor Bob! It is a shame to tease him. He must have a kind heart and an easy temper, to bury himself in the back parlour of 210 a country inn, when Audley Court is open to him.

(*Re-enter Audley with Talboys, who follows reluctantly.*)

AUDLEY. Come, come, just a peep at the *old* place, and (*Pointing with gallantry to Alice.*) the *young* beauties. My cousin, Miss Audley—Captain Talboys.

ALICE. Won't you think better of your resolve and dine with us, 215 Captain Talboys—Sir Michael will be delighted.

TALBOYS. Thank you, you're very kind; but I'm not fit company for anybody, not even for Bob.

AUDLEY. Much obliged to you for the compliment. (*To Alice.*) No, we must be back to our leg and trimmings. (*To George.*) 220 Snug, isn't it, and comfortable—what's more, none of your ghost-ridden rooms, eh. George?

---

1 *Damon ... Pythias* In Greek mythology, the two men were remarkably loyal friends.
2 *propria persona* Legal term for "for one's self."

ALICE. (*To George, who is looking round.*) You can scarcely judge of the pictures by this light. There are some good specimens of the Dutch school.[1]

AUDLEY. Ah! That's the school for a couple of boors like us, eh, George? Pipes and schnapps, churchwardens, and Schiedam.[2] Holloa! (*Pointing to portrait on chair, which is concealed with a cloth.*) What is this so mysteriously covered?

ALICE. That is the portrait of "*the most charming woman in Essex.*" It is not quite finished yet; but it is a wonderful likeness.

AUDLEY. Her portrait! By Jove! That's lucky. (*To Talboys, who is at some distance looking at a portrait on the walls.*) If you're too shy to be presented to the original, George, we must at least introduce you to the copy.

ALICE. Take care, take care. (*As Robert moves cloth.*)

AUDLEY. (*Talboys at back looking out of window as Robert looks at the portrait.*) Bravo, bravissimo! True to the life. The refinement of Raphael, with the *abandon* of Rubens.[3]

ALICE. It is an extraordinary picture, is it not?

AUDLEY. Extraordinary—it is wonderful! and yet there's something odd about it.

ALICE. There is. I've never seen exactly the expression of the canvas. (*Talboys turns to look at picture, and stands transfixed and silent—Alice and Audley converse apart, not noticing him.*)

AUDLEY. (*Taking album from table.*) My lady's album. What a pretty hand!

ALICE. You think so. I call it a scratchy scrawl.

AUDLEY. That's all your jealousy. (*Talboys casts a wild look at portrait, and goes out without being noticed by Robert and Alice.*) Such a character about it. Every trait, illustrated by a few fairy strokes. Look here, George! (*Turning round, in surprise, at Talboys' absence.*) Eh, what?

ALICE. Gone! what can be the matter?

---

1 *Dutch school* Dutch painters from the early Renaissance to the Baroque period. Among the best known are Hieronymus Bosch, Rembrandt van Rijn, and Johannes Vermeer.
2 *Schiedam* Dutch city.
3 *Raphael* Raffaello Sanzio da Urbino (1483–1520), master of the Italian High Renaissance; *Rubens* Peter Paul Rubens (1577–1640), Flemish Baroque painter known for the lushness of his works.

AUDLEY. Oh, nothing! I suppose the picture was too much for him. He has got one of his gloomy fits. He has never been the same man since his wife's death!

255 ALICE. But how strange to run off without a word.

AUDLEY. Well, we should be strange if we had suffered as he has, but I must be after him, or he'll lose himself and his dinner too, so good bye.

ALICE. Good night, Bob.

260 AUDLEY. I say Alice, you'll forgive me, won't you? It is not my fault if—if—

ALICE. If what?

AUDLEY. Why, if my aunt has the misfortune to be—

ALICE. Yes?

265 AUDLEY. "*The most charming woman in Essex.*" (*Exit Audley.*)

ALICE. Poor Bob! fluttering round the flame with the other moths. If I don't watch him he will be sure to burn his wings. (*Exit Alice.*)

(*Re-enter Lady Audley. She is in evening dress.*)

LADY A. If I were not afraid, before to-morrow's sun I would put miles between him and me. Afraid, did I say? No! courage! I will
270 be strong and brave. I have been brave to dare so much already, and I'll not falter now. Were I to play the coward I should lose all: yes, wealth, position, everything for which I have fought, ay, and suffered too. Then Phoebe! I cannot tell her this! the past is enough; she must not know the present; and—and
275 for the future I must fight my way alone. (*Pause.*) How did he know Sir Michael's nephew? I never heard him mention his name. (*Talboys enters in unobserved and stands watching her.*) It is strange that they should be such friends and—(*Seeing covering off picture—Talboys comes down so as to be close to Lady Audley*
280 *without being seen by her.*)—The covering off my portrait? Who has been here?

TALBOYS. (*In a deep firm tone.*) Your husband, Helen Talboys. (*Lady Audley utters a faint cry, but recovers, and supporting herself with one hand on a chair, looks steadily at Talboys.*) Yes, that
285 husband you swore to love and honour till—

LADY A. Death parted us. I did, I kept my word, George Talboys.
You abandoned *me*. You, of your own free will, were dead to me!

TALBOYS. What! you justify yourself, you glory in your shame?

LADY A. Shame! Who cast the shame, the bitter reproach of want
and poverty upon me? Who left me with no better protector   290
than a drunken father and the burden of a helpless child, who,
lying in his cradle, seemed, with his baby smile, to mock his
father's memory? Thank heaven he was spared his mother's
sufferings!

TALBOYS. (*In agony.*) Dead! my son dead? And I have toiled   295
and suffered for—for this. Woman, what have I done that my
reward should be this grievous wrong?

LADY A. Wrong! have not *you* wronged *me*? You prate to me of
toil and suffering. You do not know the labour that has been
my lot for many a weary day. What was my life when you   300
were gone? No helping hand held out to me by your proud
family; I, your wife, left to choose 'twixt death and drudgery.
I chose the latter, bitter though that choice was. Three years
had passed, and I had received no token of your existence, for
I knew well had you returned you would have found me under   305
any name, in any place. I argued, I reasoned, and last I *justified*
myself. I have a right to think that he is no more to me, nor I
to him, and why should I let his shadow stand between me and
prosperity?

TALBOYS. Is that all?   310

LADY A. No; to guard against detection and make assurance
doubly sure—

TALBOYS. (*Bitterly.*) I know. You needn't remind me of that. The
notice of your supposed death was my first welcome home.

LADY A. One word more, and I have done. When I became your   315
wife, George Talboys, I gave myself to you. The temptations
that wreck some had no terrors for me; nay more, though a
legion of tempters were around me I remained true to you.

TALBOYS. You may deceive yourself, you cannot deceive me. I left
you true, I return to find you false.   320

LADY A. You left me a helpless girl; you see me now a woman,
prepared to render you your due, no more.

TALBOYS. Poor child!

LADY A. Don't bring me your compassion. I've fed and battened
325 upon pity long enough to know the bitterness of such a meal.
'Tis now my turn to tender that poor dole to others. I seek
neither your aid nor sympathy. Go, forget me.

TALBOYS. And leave you to your shameless triumph. No; listen
to me, Helen Talboys, I could have forgiven all, save that one
330 passionless deliberate wrong. But now (*With determination.*) no
earthly power shall turn me from my purpose—and that is, to
drag you before the man you have deceived, and face to face
with him, tell your full tale of misery and disgrace. I'll have no
mercy without justice. (*Goes to bell.*)

335 LADY A. You will?

TALBOYS. I will. (*Going towards door.*)

LADY A. Do it, at your peril, George Talboys, do it, and I'll
denounce you before him, before this household, ay, before the
world, as a madman and a liar. Do it, and see if calumny and
340 malice can open the eyes of him who is blinded by my love.

TALBOYS. You defy me?

LADY A. I do, you want the courage or the cowardice.

TALBOYS. (*About to ring the bell—she stops him, he seizes her.*) No,
I'll respect him.

345 LADY A. You *shall* respect him. What would you have—

TALBOYS. Justice, no more! sue to the law for mercy, not to me.
(*They struggle together till they reach opening into garden by centre
window.*) I swear, if there is but one witness of your identity
living, and that witness were removed from Audley Court, by
350 the width of the whole earth, I would bring him here to swear
to, and denounce you. (*Marks creeps in and watches, as Lady
Audley and Talboys are hidden from audience.*)

MARKS. (*In a low voice.*) She defies him! Who'd a thought there
was the devil's spirit in that lily face? He threatens her; she
355 follows him—he turns again—a last word, no! a curse of bitter
hate! and now his back is turned. (*With horror.*) Ha! (*Retires
quickly by side door.*)

(*Lady Audley re-enters hurriedly—her face is deadly pale—she
casts an anxious look back, covers her face, then comes down.*)

LADY A. (*Stretching out her hands—in a wild exulting tone.*) Free, free, once more!

END OF THE FIRST ACT.

(Twelve months are supposed to have elapsed between First and Second Acts.)

ACT 2, SCENE 1

(Library at Audley Court, same as Act First, Scene Second.)

(Robert Audley discovered alone, in chair near fire-side.)

AUDLEY. (*Reading slip of paper.*) "Captain George Talboys, late of the 12th Dragoon[1] Guards.—Any person possessing any knowledge of the above, subsequent to the 7th inst., will be liberally rewarded on communicating with R. A., Chancery Lane." A year gone, and still no tidings! A year gone in trying 5
to fathom the mystery of his disappearance. This very room seems to be as gloomy as if the poor fellow had died within it. 'Twas here I last saw him alive and well; 'twas here I lost him, as suddenly as if a trap-door had opened in the solid earth and let him through to the Antipodes. (*Taking papers from pocket* 10
and reading.) "Facts and circumstantial evidence." The produce of twelve months' miserable toil. Is this paper, fashioned by the hand of no attorney, to be your first brief, Robert Audley? Why do I go on with this, when I know that it is leading me, step by step, nearer to that conclusion I would gladly shun? No, like 15
Ixion,[2] I am tied to the wheel, and must move with its every revolution: link by link I must forge the fatal chain, until the last rivet drops into its place and the circle is complete. But then, Sir Michael? My poor uncle, dying, it may be, and on *her* breast! Must I bring dishonour and disgrace on him in his hour 20

---

1   *Dragoon* Designation sometimes applied to cavalry soldiers.
2   *Ixion* In Greek mythology, Ixion was bound to a spinning wheel of fire as punishment for a series of despicable crimes.

of sickness? No; 'tis too late to turn back. Heaven help those who stand between me and the SECRET!

(*Enter Lady Audley from garden, unobserved by Audley.*)

Justice to the dead first, mercy to the living afterwards! (*Paces anxiously across the room and doesn't notice Lady Audley.*)

LADY A. All alone, Robert? Well, you seem satisfied with your
25   company.

AUDLEY. (*Turning round.*) Eh?

LADY A. (*Taking off bonnet.*) Yes; you were chattering to—to yourself most energetically.

AUDLEY. Was I? The effect, I suppose, of—

30 LADY A. Those sad habits you contract in chambers. Your life in the Temple must be a very funny, a very mysterious one.

AUDLEY. You are right, Lady Audley, it is: full of mystery, at least to me.

LADY A. (*Taking box of colours and palette, arranging easel on table*
35   *and sitting down.*) Now, please, Robert, *please* don't stalk about in that uncomfortable manner, but try and fancy this is Fig-Tree Court, and make yourself at home. Don't be afraid. (*Striking match and offering him a light.*) I don't mind your cabanas.[1]

AUDLEY. You're very good. (*Lighting cigar.*) You're quite sure the
40   smoke won't annoy you?

LADY A. Oh, no! I'm used to cigars, and pipes too. Mr. Dawson, the apothecary, where I was governess, you know, used to smoke every evening.

AUDLEY. (*Lazily.*) Did he? Good fellow, Dawson.

45 LADY A. Good! (*Laughing.*) The dearest of creatures. (*Mixing colours.*) He used to give me five and twenty pounds a year for my poor services—actually five and twenty pounds—generous little man! How well I remember receiving my salary quarterly. A wee dirty heap of gold and silver and copper, straight from
50   the surgery till, redolent of James's Powder and ipecacuanha.[2] I

---

1 *cabanas* Cigars, so named for the Spanish company that exported them.

2 *James's powder* Common fever reducer; *ipecacuanha* Root used for its laxative properties.

can't help laughing when I think of it. Why, these colours cost a guinea a-piece, in Rathbone Place. What a change!

AUDLEY. (*After a pause.*) It is a change; a metamorphosis, indeed! (*Slowly, with emphasis.*) Some women could do a great deal to accomplish such a change. (*Lady Audley starts, drops brush, and, as she picks it up, looks at him—turning cigar in his fingers.*) Won't draw; this is the third today that has played me this trick. (*Rises, and throws cigar out of window.*) I really must give my tobacconist warning. (*Returns and sits.*) 55

LADY A. Ha, ha! You're a droll, eccentric creature, Robert. Do you know, sometimes you almost puzzle me. 60

AUDLEY. Do I?

LADY A. Yes, I fancy your phantom friend, who went off in that unceremonious way, Mr.—Mr.—what was his name?

AUDLEY. George Talboys. 65

LADY A. Yes, ever since his death—

AUDLEY. Death! How do you know he is dead?

LADY A. Dear me, how you do take a poor little woman up, to be sure—just like you lawyers. Disappearance, then. Ever since that day, you've become quite a different person; I declare you're losing your good looks. 70

AUDLEY. And good manners. I'm afraid you're right.

LADY A. You'll wear yourself out, if you go on in this way. You've been half over England, haven't you, in search of him.

AUDLEY. I would go round the world, Lady Audley, to find George Talboys, or—or—his grave. 75

LADY A. Poor Pylades, you deserve to discover your Orestes.[1] I wish I could help you.

AUDLEY. There is not a seaport on our coasts where I'm not known; not an underwriter at Lloyd's or a stockbroker's clerk, who doesn't curse me for a meddling, curious fellow. At one time I had hopes of success in Yorkshire, and again I thought Southampton might enlighten me. 80

LADY A. But surely you must have arrived at some conclusion?

AUDLEY. I have. 85

---

1   *Pylades… Orestes* In Greek mythology, Pylades was extremely loyal to his cousin Orestes and helped him avenge his father's murder.

LADY A. I thought so.

AUDLEY. Through the thick mist I can still grope my way to one supposition, to one certainty.

LADY A. And that is?

90 AUDLEY. That George Talboys never went into Yorkshire or Southampton, that is all.

LADY A. But you once told me you had traced him to the latter place, that you had seen his father-in-law—more, that his father-in-law had seen *him*.

95 AUDLEY. True; but I have reason to doubt that gentleman's integrity.

LADY A. What do you mean?

AUDLEY. Have you ever studied any work on evidence, Lady Audley? Best or Starkie, or Taylor,[1] for instance—I suppose not.
100 *I* have.

LADY A. Then I don't give up all hopes of seeing you on the woolsack after all. And your acquaintance with these legal luminaries—

AUDLEY. Has determined me to discredit the word of any man or
105 *woman*, unless confirmed by proof.

LADY A. Oh, indeed! Then for the sake of your peace of mind, and the character of the male and female community generally, the sooner you discard these worthies the better, Robert Audley.

AUDLEY. Hear me out, please. Sir Michael may have told you
110 I have never practised as a barrister, that I have shrunk, not through fear of incapacity, but from sheer inactivity from the responsibilities of my profession—that is not far from the truth; but we are sometimes FORCED into the position we have most avoided, and I have of late found myself compelled to turn my
115 attention to the study of the CRIMINAL law.

LADY A. Dear me, why you are quite a detective. I wonder with your suspicious tendencies, you have not enrolled yourself at Scotland Yard.[2]

---

1 *Best* William Mawdesley Best (1809–69), author of *The principles of the law of evidence with elementary rules for conducting the examination and cross-examination of witnesses*; *Starkie* Thomas Starkie (1782–1849), author of *A Practical Treatise on the Law of Evidence*; *Taylor* Edgar Taylor (1793–1839), author of *The Book of Rights*.
2 *Scotland Yard* Headquarters of the Metropolitan Police Service in London.

AUDLEY. I wish I had, Lady Audley, rather than have entered my
uncle's house during the past year.   120

LADY A. If you will insist in talking in enigmas, you must excuse
me if I fail to understand you. I have been playing at *patience*
for some time—

AUDLEY. And now, in our little *écarté*[1] duet, you expect me to
throw down my cards. Well, you may see my hand—I leave   125
proposal or refusal to you.

LADY A. Thank you, you are very generous, but you get hazier
than ever. Ha, ha! I'm sure that cigar must have been a bad one.

AUDLEY. Let me try to make myself plain. George Talboys—

LADY A. *Toujours perdrix.*[2] My dear Robert, cannot you find any   130
other subject for conversation?

AUDLEY. No, Lady Audley, none so fitting for the present season.
(*Draws chair nearer Lady Audley.*) Listen! A year has elapsed
since the insertion of this advertisement. (*Produces slip of paper.*)

LADY A. I remember, I am not likely to forget it—it figured at   135
the head of the second column of the *Times*, all last season; it is
a credit to your grammar and orthography, but it has resulted
in nothing.

AUDLEY. Pardon me; it has resulted in the belief of my friend's
death, and—   140

LADY A. Exactly, just as I told you, and—

AUDLEY. In the consequent examination, by me, of the effects he
left in my chambers.

LADY A. Indeed! and they are, I presume, coats, waistcoats,
patent leather boots, meerschaum pipes,[3] worked slippers with   145
the beads tumbling off, opera orders, and—

AUDLEY. And *letters*.

LADY A. Of course, the usual rubbish, sanctified by time; a heap
of letters from his old schoolfellows, his brother officers—

AUDLEY. And *his wife*.   150

---

1 *écarté* Card game played by two people, in which players may discard part of their
   hands in exchange for new cards.

2 *Toujours perdrix* French phrase, literally meaning "always partridge" and figuratively
   suggesting "too much of a good thing."

3 *meerschaum pipe* Smoking tobacco pipe crafted from meerschaum, a clay-like mineral.

LADY A. His wife! (*Satirically.*) And you have been amusing yourself with laughing over poor Phyllis's amatory platitudes. Oh, fie! Mr. Audley, fie!

AUDLEY. I have done nothing of the kind. (*Taking packet of letters from breast pocket.*) See, the seal upon the string remains unbroken. (*Looks anxiously at packet—changing his tone and manner.*) Talking of letters, what a pretty hand *you* write, Lady Audley. (*Puts back packet in pocket.*)

LADY A. Do I? To set good copies, is, you know, one of the chief qualifications of a governess. You have remarked my handwriting?

AUDLEY. I have, often. (*Draws chair closer.*) I should know it among a thousand.

LADY A. (*Pause.*) And you still persist in this wild chase. (*Rises.*) Well, every one to his taste. Now take my advice, Robert, and shake off this morbid fancy; try change of air; take a good run on the Continent.

AUDLEY. For my own sake, I wish I could; but I must stay where duty bids me.

LADY A. And that is?

AUDLEY. Here, in this house; or, if my society is distasteful, in the neighbourhood.

LADY A. I understand. You are anxious about Sir Michael's health: very natural, your devotion does you credit. (*Puts brushes and colours in box.*)

AUDLEY. (*Impressively.*) There is no one, to whom my uncle's life can be of more value than to *you*, Lady Audley. Your happiness, your prosperity, in a word your *safety* depends on his existence. (*Rises.*)

LADY A. (*Looking fixedly at Audley.*) Yes, I know that as well as you. At his death, envy and malice must be my portion; but while he lives, they who strike *me*, must strike through *him*. (*With change of manner.*) Oh! here comes Sir Michael and Alice, so good-bye for the present to our little *tête-à-tête*. (*As Audley goes.*) I wish with all my heart, Mr. Audley, you could discover your poor friend, it would make us all cheerful once more.

AUDLEY. I'm not so sure of that. (*Aside.*) The circle lessens day by day. Yes; George Talboys never left Audley Court. At our next meeting it must be justice and not pity. (*Exit.*) 190

LADY A. (*Alone.*) He remain here! No; not while I am mistress of this house. I'll speak to Sir Michael at once. He can gainsay me nothing, and Alice's jealousy will but serve to aid my purpose. Stay! these letters once in my possession, I could defy him—but how to obtain them? Phoebe, yes, *she* must help me. (*Going to* 195 *window, assisting Sir Michael, who enters, leaning on Alice's arm; he looks pale and ill.*)

ALICE. (*Aside, quitting Sir Michael.*) Robert here with her! always with her. (*Exit.*)

LADY A. (*To Sir Michael.*) You look tired, love! You shouldn't have stayed out so long.

SIR M. The fresh air does me good, Lucy. I fret like a caged bird 200 without it. Didn't I see Bob here just now?

LADY A. Yes; Mr. Audley has been honouring me with his society half the day. How long is he going to stay with us?

SIR M. How long? Why as long as he pleases—till he is tired of us, I suppose. Bob is always welcome here. Why do you ask, 205 darling?

LADY A. Oh! I don't know—I was only thinking.

SIR M. I see, I see; you're getting bored with his lazy habits, kicking about the damask ottoman as if he was at his club. And then his cigars— 210

LADY A. Oh! no, no, it isn't that exactly; the fact is, dear, you won't be angry if I speak plainly, Robert Audley is very agreeable, very agreeable indeed, but you must remember I am *rather* a young aunt for such a nephew—and—

SIR M. And what, Lucy? 215

LADY A. Why our dear Alice is a little jealous of any trifling attention Mr. Audley pays me, and—and I think it would perhaps be better for her happiness if—if, in short, his visit were brought to a close.

SIR M. (*Aside.*) What have I been about not to have thought of 220 this before? (*Aloud.*) He shall go to-night, Lucy, to-night.

LADY A. Oh, no!

SIR M. But I say yes, to-night. I've been a blind old fool; not but
that Bob is as honest and true-hearted a fellow as ever breathed,
225   but—but he shall go to-night, Lucy, to-night.

LADY A. But don't be rude to him, love; you won't, will you?

SIR M. Rude to him! to Bob? Don't be afraid. Bob is as easy as
an old shoe. He'll take a hint from me. There he goes, puffing
his eternal cigar, on the terrace. I'll tackle him at once; don't be
230   alarmed, you can't offend him. Why, Bob, bless you, my love,
Bob Audley is as simple as a child. (*Exit.*)

LADY A. "Simple as a child!" Poor Sir Michael, you want a glass
through which to read your nephew. *Simple!* he's as cunning as
a fox; but in the boastful moment of success you have shown
235   me your cards, Robert Audley, and thanks to your courtesy, you
have taught me how win the game. (*Exit.*)

(*Enter Alice.*)

ALICE. (*Alone.*) The vain, frivolous, heartless coquette. He has
been at her feet half the day; he is captivated, ensnared by
the little soft hands, and the large eyes, and all the fantastical
240   nonsense which men and fools call fascination. I hate her! I
can't help it—I *do hate* her; hasn't she come between father and
daughter, and tried to rob poor Alice of the love of that dear
generous heart? And now, isn't she employing her arts and wiles
to lure him? I shall hate *him* next! Yesterday, he little thought I
245   noticed him, he turned as pale as a sheet when he met her. Yes,
it must be for her sake that he has been moping and mooning,
and of late has become such a disconsolate object. It cannot be
passion. No, it is his innate eccentricity, that's what it is. Yes,
Bob Audley is just the very sort of man to fall in love with his
250   aunt. (*Seeing Audley coming from garden she sits down, takes up a
book and pretends to be absorbed in it as Audley enters and comes
behind her chair.*)

AUDLEY. Well, cousin? Reading?

ALICE. (*without looking up.*) Changes and Chances.

AUDLEY. A novel?

ALICE. Yes.

255   AUDLEY. Who is it by?

ALICE. The author of *Shuffles and Subterfuges*.

AUDLEY. Ah! is it interesting?

ALICE. No.

AUDLEY. Instructive?

ALICE. Quite the reverse. 260

AUDLEY. In that case, as I am off in ten minutes, perhaps you'll condescend to give me five of your society?

ALICE. (*Putting down book and rising.*) Off! where?

AUDLEY. Out of this house—I've notice to quit.

ALICE. I don't understand you; who has— 265

AUDLEY. Your father—my uncle; and his word, you know, is as good as his bond.

ALICE. (*Aside.*) Then I was right! My poor father! His suspicions are at length aroused. (*Aloud to Audley.*) He is quite right, Bob, quite right, and I am very glad you're going. 270

AUDLEY. The deuce you are?

ALICE. You're doing no good here, Bob. You're fit for nothing now but to hold a skein of silk, or read Tennyson[1] to Lady Audley.

AUDLEY. Alice, don't be ridiculous! My aunt interests me, that's my reason for courting her company. 275

ALICE. Oh! (*Pointedly.*) and some other people *don't* interest you, that's what you mean?

AUDLEY. I mean no such thing. Why will you go off in that neck-or-nothing[2] style? A conclusion is not a five-barred gate, you needn't rush at it. Now don't be angry, we've not much time left 280 for quarrelling.

ALICE. But why are you going in such a hurry?

AUDLEY. I've told you, because Sir Michael wishes me to leave this house; but I shan't be far off, I shall stay—

ALICE. At the "Audley Arms," I suppose? 285

AUDLEY. No, not at the "Audley Arms": in—in the neighbourhood.

ALICE. (*Aside.*) He cannot tear himself from her.

AUDLEY. I wish to be within hail. Your father, Alice, is very ill, he is sadly broken.

---

1 *Tennyson* Alfred, Lord Tennyson (1809–92), perhaps the most popular of Victorian poets and Poet Laureate from 1850 until his death.

2 *neck-or-nothing* Determined, heedless of risk.

290   ALICE. (*Aside.*) Can he be playing the hypocrite? (*Aloud.*) You think papa altered?

AUDLEY. Altered! he's breaking fast. If anything should happen to him, I should wish to be near Audley Court, near—near you, Alice, ready to hold out the hand of aid and sympathy.

295   ALICE. You're very kind, Bob, very.

AUDLEY. No, I'm only anxious to give you my best advice. If you won't be in a hurry to run off with the first fox-hunting baronet who comes in your way; if you'll only be patient, Alice, and ride across country with a little less—what shall I say?—*splash*, and a

300   little more *judgment*, I have no doubt the *person* you prefer will, in the end, make you a very excellent husband.

ALICE. Thank you, cousin; but, as you may not know the person I prefer, perhaps you'd better not take it upon yourself to answer for him or me. (*Aside, sobbing.*) Can he love her?

305   AUDLEY. What, Alice!

ALICE. (*Sobbing, aside.*) He dare not love her!

AUDLEY. Alice, my darling, in tears! What, what is the matter?

ALICE. N—nothing, it—it's only the feather of my hat that got into my eye. Good-bye, Bob! (*Shaking hands.*) good-bye!

310   (*Aside.*) In love with *her*! I won't believe it. (*Exit quickly.*)

AUDLEY. Poor little soul! (*Looking off.*) The green-eyed monster has got her tight in his clutches. Yes, she is jealous—jealous, I do believe, of her stepmother, and—and me. (*Looks out of window.*) There she goes off for a gallop, ready to break her heart

315   and her neck too. Silly child! What a figure! What a seat! What a hand on the bridle, as light as a feather! I wonder whether she'll manage her husband as easily as she does her horse? Yes, woman's a riddle—a riddle that I have not solved yet. By Jove, I think that if I ever marry, and have any daughters, they shall

320   be educated in Paper Buildings, take their daily walks in the Temple Gardens, and never go beyond the Porter's Lodge till the morning on which they're carried to St. Dunstan's or St. Bride's,[1] and served with a *conjugal attachment*. (*Exit.*)

---

1   *Paper Buildings* Law office complex in the Temple district; *Porter's Lodge* Here, administrative office at the entrance to one of the Inns of Court; *St. Dunstan's or St. Bride's* Churches just outside the Temple district.

ACT 2, Scene 2

(Exterior of the "Chequers" Inn, Mount Stanning; twilight.)

(Enter Marks, partly intoxicated, followed by Phoebe.)

MARKS. What are you whimpering for? I tell you the fellow won't budge. I've tried to get over him with drink, to blow his head off with blue ruin,[1] but it's no go. He'd drain the river if it ran Hollands.[2] I tell you gal, he won't give up possession without the money.   5

PHOEBE. But what are we to do, Luke? Where's the money to come from?

MARKS. Come from? Why, from the same place, the same person it did before. I'll not be turned out o' house and home for a—

PHOEBE. Hush, Luke, hush! You're not sober, you don't know   10 what you are saying.

MARKS. I'm not so drunk as that, don't think it.

PHOEBE. I told her of our distress last night, and she promised to help us.

MARKS. And she shall keep her word.   15

PHOEBE. But you know how much she has done for us already, Luke—how kind she has been.

MARKS. Kind! ugh! hang her kindness, 'taint that we want, it's her *money*. She won't get no snivellin' gratitude out o' me, I can tell you. Whatever she does she does because she's obliged, and if   20 she warn't obliged she wouldn't do it.

PHOEBE. If we could only get rid of this place, Luke, sell the goodwill[3]—

MARKS. Goodwill! Ha, ha! The goodwill of this rotten crazy pile, what would that fetch without my lady's secret.   25

PHOEBE. Hush, hush! I heard a footstep; there's somebody at the wicket.

MARKS. Another cursed bailiff. Go and see who it is; if—if it's a

---

1 *blue ruin* Poor-quality gin.

2 *Hollands* Gin made in Holland.

3 *goodwill* In commercial sales, the right to make use of a business's established reputation.

30

35

40

45

50

customer, there's not much for him, hardly a gallon left. (*Exit Phoebe.*) We've turned a penny out o' Phoebe's secret; if my lady won't help us, I will see what mine'll fetch. (*Phoebe returns followed by Audley—aside.*) The counsellor! What does he want with us, and at this hour? (*Aloud.*) Servant, Mr. Audley.

AUDLEY. I've a favour to ask of you, Mr. Marks, and of your good wife; the favour of bed and board for a few days.

MARKS. You're welcome, sir, to anything, (*Aside.*) by paying.

AUDLEY. I'm easily satisfied; a shake-down[1] and a bit o' supper are all my wants to-night.

MARKS. Supper, there ain't much in the house except a sheriff's officer. I wish somebody 'ud eat him; they'd find him tough enough.

AUDLEY. In difficulties, eh, Marks? That's bad news. Come, come, you must tell me all, over your pipe and a mug of ale, within; I've tobacco enough for both of us.

PHOEBE. That way, then, if you please, sir. (*Exit Audley.*) (*To Marks, in an under-tone.*) Keep yourself in your senses, Luke. (*Exit Phoebe after Audley.*)

MARKS. Ay, ay! You mind your own business, and leave me to mine. What's his game? There's mischief brewin', I'll bet a crown. Drunk, am I? I—I ain't too drunk to see a hole in a ladder; I ain't too drunk to swear that our fine gentleman will turn out an ugly customer. (*Exit.*)

ACT 2, SCENE 3

(*Interior of the "Chequers" Inn; Countrymen drinking and smoking; fire burning on hearth; table with candles alight on it.*)

(*Enter Audley and Phoebe.*)

PHOEBE. (*Pointing to Men drinking.*) They'll be gone directly sir; we have but this room furnished now.

---

1   *shake-down* Straw bed placed on the floor; more generally, improvised bed, especially when arranged on the floor.

AUDLEY. Don't let me disturb them. (*Watching Phoebe as she lays the cloth on table and prepares supper—aside.*) I would give something to know what's passing in the mind of my pale hostess at this moment. That cold, gray face could tell a tale, or I am much mistaken. That's just my idea of a woman who could keep a secret. 5

PHOEBE. You've come straight from the Court, I suppose, sir?

AUDLEY. Not very long ago; this afternoon. 10

PHOEBE. And Sir Michael, poor gentleman, is he better?

AUDLEY. I fear not.

PHOEBE. And my lady, was she quite well?

AUDLEY. Quite well. (*To Phoebe, going.*) Stay, Mrs. Marks, one moment. You knew Lady Audley, did you not, before her marriage, when she was— 15

PHOEBE. (*Quickly.*) Miss Graham. Oh, yes, sir! I lived at Mr. Dawson's the apothecary's when Miss Graham—I mean when my lady—was governess there.

AUDLEY. Indeed! Was she long at Mr. Dawson's? 20

PHOEBE. Near upon two years, sir.

AUDLEY. And she came from London?

PHOEBE. Yes, sir, so I have heard say.

AUDLEY. And was an orphan. I believe.

PHOEBE. I believe so, sir. (*Going.*) 25

AUDLEY. Always as gay and lighthearted as now?

PHOEBE. Always, sir.

AUDLEY. Ah! (*Aside.*) She'd be as firm as a rock in the witness-box. How she would bother Badger in cross-examination.

PHOEBE. Ah! (*Aside.*) What can be his purpose? If there's any bad meaning in his coming, my lady must know of it. 30

COUNTRYMEN. (*To Marks, who enters.*) Good night, Master Luke!

MARKS. Good night, Joe—good night, Simon! (*Exeunt Countrymen.*) (*To Audley.*) It's very rough for such fine folks as you, Mr. Audley, Eh! what—why, what's this stuff? Tea! ugh! damp gunpowder! Give us something with fire in it. Give us the bottle, gal—(*Sits opposite Audley.*) give us the bottle. 35

PHOEBE. (*To Marks, in an under-tone.*) Not tonight, Luke, not tonight, for heaven's sake.

40 MARKS. Fetch it, I say—d'ye hear me? 'Taint often we've quality
company here, and I'm going to settle down for a comfortable
smoke.

PHOEBE. (*Making signs to Marks.*) We—we forgot the brewhouse
door. Will you come and help me put up the bar?

45 MARKS. No, I shan't stir, there—I ain't a-going to move, I tell
you. (*Drinking.*) Put the bar up yourself.

PHOEBE. But it's too heavy for me to lift.

MARKS. Then let the bar bide! You're mighty careful o' that
brewhouse door, all of a sudden, you are! I suppose you're afraid

50 I should open my mouth to Mr. Robert here. You're always
clipping off my words before they're out; but I won't stand
it—d'ye hear, *I won't stand it!*

AUDLEY. (*Aside.*) She daren't leave him. Could that pale face help
me in my search for him? No, no. This is a change from the

55 club smoking-room, and yet this drunken brute's society has
a charm for me. (*Aloud.*) The wind's getting up, and it is not
over warm within, notwithstanding your cheerful blaze. A man
wants something to keep the cold out. (*To Marks.*) Your glass
is empty.

60 MARKS. The wind goes right through the house as if it was a sieve.
I've had the rheumaticks[1] ever since we came here.

AUDLEY. Yes, it is a poor place. You, with your interest at Audley
Court, might have done better, surely!

MARKS. Better!—if folks hadn't been so stingy, I might have had

65 a public at Brentwood or Chelmsford, instead o' this old rotten
crib. What's fifty pounds? What's a hundred pounds—

PHOEBE. (*In a low voice.*) Luke, Luke!

MARKS. No, you don't stop me with all your Lukes. (*Louder.*) I
say—what's a hundred pounds—

70 AUDLEY. What indeed, to a man like you, possessed of the power
you and your wife hold over the *person* in question?

MARKS. What! you know?

AUDLEY. More than some people give me credit for.

MARKS. But you want to know more still, eh, Mr. Counsellor?

75 (*Aside.*) He's not such a fool as I thought him, after all.

---

1   *rheumaticks* Joint or muscular pains, akin to arthritis.

AUDLEY. "Knowledge," as the copybook[1] tells us, "is power."

MARKS. And what's more, knowledge may be had by paying for it—paying for it handsomely. (*Bell rings.*) Eh—

PHOEBE. The bell! Who can that be?

MARKS. Go out and see. (*Phoebe runs out quickly.*) If it's another gentleman with the sheriff's card, tell him we've got an execution in the house already, and if he comes, mayhap there'll be a murder too.   80

AUDLEY. (*Aside.*) He wants money sadly, and would sell his soul for a barrel of ale. But how can I depend upon him? Audley is a richer mine to work than Fig-Tree Court.   85

(*Phoebe returns agitated and whispers to Marks.*)

MARKS. What! she here? at this time o' night, and walked, d'ye say?

PHOEBE. The whole way, and alone. It's about the rent, she couldn't bear to think we were in trouble. (*Exit.*)   90

AUDLEY. (*Aside.*) Late hours, indeed, for an autumn walk, Lady Audley! Nothing but an action of charity could be the motive for such a rash proceeding. (*Aloud.*) Well, good night, my worthy hosts. (*Aside.*) I wonder whether there's a lock to my door? (*Aloud.*) I'll send up to the Court to-morrow for my traps.   95
Hot water, please, at half-past eight. Good night. (*Exit.*)

PHOEBE. (*To Marks, earnestly, as Lady Audley enters.*) Keep sober for a few minutes, Luke, if you don't wish to ruin us.

MARKS. What's her business here?

LADY A. My business, Luke Marks, is to pay your debt, not for your sake, but for your wretched wife's.   100

MARKS. You might a' sent the money to Phoebe. We don't want no fine ladies pryin' here, pokin' their noses into our affairs.

PHOEBE. Oh, Luke! for mercy's sake—

LADY A. I am not here to listen to your insolence, Luke Marks. How much is the debt?   105

MARKS. Nine pun' odd.

---

1   *copybook* Allusive term for proverbial wisdom.

LADY A. There are ten pounds. Now go; I have something to say to your wife.

110 MARKS. (*Going—aside.*) Bark, bark away, my lady, but have a care. I've shown my teeth 'fore now, and the next time I'll bite. (*Exit.*)

PHOEBE. You are not going back alone, my lady?

LADY A. Why not? I came alone.

115 PHOEBE. But you will let me go with you?

LADY A. And leave those men together?

PHOEBE. He's gone to rest, my lady; not a word has passed except while I was by.

LADY A. And he sleeps here to-night?

120 PHOEBE. In the front room, my lady.

LADY A. (*Aside.*) The front room!

PHOEBE. He may be in bed by this time; he told us he is going to stay some days.

LADY A. Some days! (*Aside.*) Yes, he'll do it; he'll keep his word
125 to—to his dear friend, unless some strange calamity befalls him, and stills his tongue for ever.

PHOEBE. I'll give you a receipt, my lady, and put Luke safe away. If I wasn't to look after him, heaven knows what might happen; we might be burnt in our beds. (*Exit.*)

130 LADY A. *Burnt in their beds! He* sleeps in the front room. Why this old lath and plaster house would burn like tinder in a moment. (*Pause.*) Those letters still in his keeping. If I were to—I was not wicked when I was young. My worst crime was the impulse of the hour. Dare I defy him? Dare I? Will he stay his hand now
135 that he has gone so far? Will anything stay it but—but *death?*

(*Phoebe re-enters.*)

PHOEBE. Here is the receipt. How pale, how ill you look, my lady.

LADY A. I am ill, child. Some water, Phoebe.

PHOEBE. There is a well outside.

LADY A. (*Shuddering.*) A well! No, no, not there. Some water,
140 child, to bathe my face.

PHOEBE. Yes, my lady, in the spare room.

LADY A. Where did you say he—Mr. Audley, sleeps?

PHOEBE. In the front room.

LADY A. Give me a candle, quick! (*To Phoebe who is following her—authoritatively.*) Stay where you are! (*Exit.*) 145

PHOEBE. Poor soul! she trusts me still. Why did I ever marry Luke? Because I feared him; often and often, I've made up the very sentence I meant to say to him, but I dared not give it utterance. I've watched, and watched him, as he has sat on the stile trimming a hedge-stake with his big clasp knife, till I have 150 thought he was just one of those who decoyed their sweethearts into lonely places, and murdered them for—

LADY A. (*Returning without candle.*) Phoebe!

PHOEBE. (*Trembling.*) Ye—yes, my lady.

LADY A. I am ready, come— 155

PHOEBE. But the light, you've left it—

LADY A. The wind blew it out on—on the stairs!

PHOEBE. The stairs?

LADY A. Yes, yes.

PHOEBE. Are you sure it was quite out, my lady? 160

LADY A. (*Impatiently.*) I tell you, yes. Why do you worry me with such a trifle? Don't you see I'm shivering! Come, Phoebe, come! (*Exeunt Lady Audley and Phoebe.*)

ACT 2, SCENE 4

(*Woody Landscape.*)

(*Enter Lady Audley followed by Phoebe.*)

LADY A. Keep close beside me, Phoebe. (*Looking anxiously back.*)

PHOEBE. Why do you look back, my lady?

LADY A. (*Aside.*) I dare not look back. (*Aloud.*) What noise was that?

PHOEBE. Only the wind among the trees, my lady. 5

LADY A. How weary the way seems! Each minute is an hour!

PHOEBE. See, yonder light?

LADY A. (*Anxiously.*) The light! Where? where?

PHOEBE. At the park gates; but a few minutes more and we shall be there, safe. 10

LADY A. Yes, yes, we *shall* be *safe.*

PHOEBE. The storm has almost ceased.

LADY A. (*Aside, in a low voice, touching her heart.*) No, no, not the storm *here*, it rages still. Come, child, come.

15 PHOEBE. (*Taking Lady Audley's hand.*) How cold your hand is my lady! It is like marble!

LADY A. As my heart. (*Exeunt Lady Audley and Phoebe.*)

ACT 2, Scene 5

(*The Lime Walk; View of Audley Court at back; lights in the window; The Ruined Well; moonlight.*)

(*Enter Lady Audley and Phoebe.*)

LADY A. At home at last; the mile has seemed a league. Phoebe, you shall stay here to-night.

PHOEBE. Oh! my lady, I daren't. I can't leave Luke alone.

LADY A. Why not? Is his life so precious?

5 PHOEBE. It isn't that, my lady, but—

LADY A. But what, child?

PHOEBE. I must go back.

LADY A. And I say, you must not. My mind is made up. To-night you stay at Audley Court.

10 PHOEBE. Oh! but I must go back, my lady, I forgot—

LADY A. What!

PHOEBE. That Mr. Audley was—(*Starting—seeing reflection of the distant flames.*) Oh! great heavens! What's that, my lady? See, there, and there again!

15 LADY A. Well, child, I see, what of it?

PHOEBE. The fire!—look, the fire!

LADY A. Fire! So it is; dear, dear, at Brentwood, or further still, quite in the distance.

PHOEBE. Oh, no, my lady, nearer, nearer than that. It is in the
20 direction of Mount Stanning.

LADY A. Nonsense, you silly child; 'tis the reflection that deceives you; 'tis miles, miles away.

PHOEBE. No, no, it is at Mount Stanning! I thought of fire to-
night—when, when—I shouldn't care for the house, my lady,
but there's Luke too tipsy to help himself—and Mr.—   25

LADY A. Are you mad? (*Seizing Phoebe's hand with force.*)

PHOEBE. (*On her knees.*) Oh, my lady! say it is not true! it is too—
too horrible!

LADY A. What is too horrible? What do you mean?

PHOEBE. Forgive me if I'm wrong. Why did you come to us to-   30
night? You, who are so bitter against Luke—and against him—
oh, speak, my lady, tell me I'm doing you a wicked wrong.

LADY A. I'll tell you nothing. Get up, fool! idiot! coward! What is
Robert Audley to you? How do you know the fire is at Mount
Stanning? You see a red patch in the sky, and straight cry out   35
your wretched hovel is in flames, as if no other place could be
burnt save that. Get up, woman. (*Phoebe rises, trembling.*) Go
back, look after your goods, your drunken husband and your
lodger. Get up and go.

PHOEBE. Oh, my lady! Forgive me! forgive me. I don't mind your   40
cruel words, but—(*Listening.*)—ah! (*Distant voices heard.*) See,
the flames burst out again, and now—yes—by the line of that
oak tree I know the spot—

LADY A. (*Looking fixedly at fire.*) It is the inn, your home.

PHOEBE. (*In accents of wild terror.*) Then he is lost! (*Exit quickly.*)   45

LADY A. (*Watching fire triumphantly.*) And I am saved! (*She
continues watching the fire for a few moments, then, wrapping
hood and cloak round her, goes towards house—as she passes the
Ruined Well, Robert Audley comes down suddenly, and confronts
her—she starts, looks at him wildly, and then gradually lapses into
a cold, impassive manner.*)

AUDLEY. You here. Lady Audley?

LADY A. Yes; (*Hesitating.*) I came out to see the—

AUDLEY. The miserable work of your own hands. Nay, you cannot
deceive me, Lady Audley. I gave you fair warning, you rejected   50
it; the time is now past for tenderness and pity.

LADY A. Let me pass, sir!

AUDLEY. No; I must speak. There is no better spot than this for
what I have to say.

LADY A. Why do you stay me here in this haunted walk?   55

AUDLEY. Yes, haunted in your eyes by the ghost of George Talboys.

LADY A. What is George Talboys to me? Once more, sir, let me pass.

AUDLEY. No, you *shall* listen. I was a witness of the joyful pride with which poor George looked forward to his reunion with his
60 wife, and I was a witness too of the blow which struck him to the heart, the announcement of her death. I now believe that announcement was a black and bitter lie.

LADY A. Indeed!

AUDLEY. Ay, and more than that, a conspiracy carried out by
65 Helen Talboys and her father—

LADY A. You have a fertile imagination, Mr. Audley.

AUDLEY. A conspiracy planned by an artful girl, who had taken advantage of poor George's absence to win another and a richer husband; a heartless, shameless woman, who speculated on the
70 chances of his death, and seized wealth and station at the risk of a base and hideous crime.

LADY A. Despite the cold, your energy interests me. I thought you told me Captain Talboys saw his wife's grave in Ventnor churchyard?

75 AUDLEY. I did, but I have reason to believe that Helen Talboys was never buried, that she was alive then, is living now. I have sworn to unravel the mystery of my poor friend's death, and I will spare neither myself nor others pain or grief unless—

LADY A. (*Eagerly.*) Unless what?

80 AUDLEY. Unless the woman I would save from disgrace and punishment accepts the terms I offer her while there is yet time.

LADY A. She would be a very foolish woman if she suffered herself to be influenced by any such absurdity. For the last time let me pass!

85 AUDLEY. No, Lady Audley, I have given you indirect warning of your danger.

LADY A. My danger! what do you mean?

AUDLEY. This—Helen Talboys left her father's house on the 16th of August, 1850; a month from that date she re-appeared not a
90 mile from where we are now standing, as—Lucy Graham.

LADY A. What does this story prove?

AUDLEY. By itself, little, but with the help of other evidence, the evidence of two labels, pasted one over the other on a box,

once yours, obtained by me from Mr. Dawson and now in my
possession, the upper label bearing the name of Miss Graham, 95
the lower, that of Mrs. Talboys! (*Lady Audley clasps her hands
convulsively, and clings to wall of Well for support—aside.*) The
shot has gone home! Heaven help her now!

LADY A. (*Regaining her self-possession.*) Robert Audley! were I
standing in the felon's dock, I might have cause perhaps to dread 100
your accusing tongue, but, as it is, I can afford to laugh with
pity at your crazy tale. If you please to say that Helen Talboys is
not dead, and that I am Helen Talboys, do so. If you choose to
wander to and fro, haunting the places she and I by common
chance have visited alike, follow your silly bent; but, let me tell 105
you, that such fancies have ere this conducted many a man,
with a less clouded brain than yours, to the life-long prison of
a mad house.

AUDLEY. You defy me?

LADY A. I do. 110

AUDLEY. Then 'tis a duel?

LADY A. *To the death!* (*Bell rings, voices heard, lights seen.*)

(*Enter Alice overwhelmed with grief; on seeing Lady Audley she
stops suddenly.*)

AUDLEY. (*Listening to bell.*) That sound!

ALICE. (*Aside.*) He here! with her!

AUDLEY. Alice, what does this mean? 115

ALICE. (*Reproachfully to Lady Audley.*) His last words were for you!

AUDLEY. His last words! What do I hear? Alice—Sir
Michael—dead?

ALICE. He asked for both of you. With his passing breath he
called for—for his wife, but there was no reply. 120

LADY A. (*Aside.*) The last hope fled! Sir Michael gone? Then he
will not forbear.

AUDLEY. Dead! my uncle dead? Then he has been spared the worst.

ALICE. The worst! what do you mean? Cousin, why are you here
at this hour, and with her? 125

AUDLEY. Alice, I have sworn to bring the murderer of George
Talboys to justice, and I will keep my oath. 'Twas by her hands

that my friend met his death. George Talboys was last seen entering these gardens by that gate, (*Pointing.*) but he was never

130   seen to leave them. Belief, nay, more, conviction cries to me, his body lies hidden in some forgotten place; ay, (*To Lady Audley, who laughs sardonically.*) you may laugh and scoff, but I'll have such a search made as shall level the old house to the ground, nor will I stay the pick or spade save at the grave's mouth of my

135   murdered friend.

LADY A. You shall not live to do it. I'd kill you first. What have I done to you, Robert Audley, that you elect yourself my persecutor? What have I done that you should dog my steps, should watch my looks, and play the spy upon me? Coward!

140   But you know not what it is to wrestle with me. Alone, unaided, I defy you, Robert Audley! Be judge, approver, all, bring forth your witnesses!

VOICES. (*Without.*) It's not too late. It's not too late.

(*Enter Peasants bearing Marks on a rude litter; Phoebe, by the side of the litter, weeping; a crowd of Countrymen and Women following.*)

MARKS. (*Feebly.*) Lay me down, lay me down. She here! (*Looking*

145   *at Lady Audley.*) Then it's not too late. (*The litter is put down, the Peasants group round the Well, so as to shut it from the Audience.*)

PHOEBE. (*Bending over Marks.*) Luke, you wouldn't say anything against those who have been so good and kind to you and me?

MARKS. (*Raising himself.*) I shall say what I please, girl. You ain't the parson nor the lawyer neither. (*To Lady Audley.*) What I

150   am now, I owe to your quick hand and ready match. What I may be, (*Turning to Audley.*) I owe to you. You did your best to save what wasn't worth the saving—the life of a poor drunken wretch. I—I'm obliged to you.

AUDLEY. I need no thanks, Luke Marks. I'm glad I was of service.

155 MARKS. You was uncommon fond o' that friend of yours, as disappeared here about a year ago, wasn't you, sir?

PHOEBE. Hush, pray be silent, Luke!

MARKS. I'll not be silent. I say you was very fond o' that Captain Talboys.

AUDLEY. Well, well? 160

LADY A. (*To Phoebe.*) Can nothing stop his tongue? (*Aloud.*) Poor
fellow! his mind is wandering.

MARKS. You're right, my lady, it is; wandering with you a twelve
months' back beneath these limes—wandering along with him.

PHOEBE. Luke, Luke! what is it you are talking of? 165

MARKS. I'm goin' to tell you. Give me some water—quick! I'm
faint—lift me. You—(*To Lady Audley.*) you little thought! I
watched you while you two were bandying harsh words and
threats, and worse than that. You little thought I was beneath
the shade of yonder window and saw her, (*Pointing to Lady* 170
Audley.) as he leant against the windlass[1] of the well, draw out
the rusty spindle from the shrunken socket, and when he fell
into the black gulf—

ALL. Ah! (*Cries of horror.*)

MARKS. I say, you little thought I crouched and listened and 175
heard, as you ran back, your cry of triumph: "Free! free! once
more!"

LADY A. You lie, Luke Marks, you lie!—the proof! the proof!

MARKS. The proof—you want the proof? (*Motioning to the
Bystanders to retire from Well, and pointing to Talboys, who has* 180
been hitherto concealed by the Crowd.) There!

(*Lady Audley totters and is supported by Phoebe— she keeps her
eyes fixed on Talboys.*)

AUDLEY. George, my dear friend, alive! (*Embracing Talboys.*) Oh,
George! I would welcome another year of agony to buy this
moment's joy. And this man's tale—

TALBOYS. Is true. The fellow kept his secret and traded on it; he 185
broke his word to me by not delivering a letter which might
have saved her much. (*Pointing to Lady Audley.*) But I'll not
blame him now; 'twas he that gave me life; 'twas his strong arm
that stayed the hand of death.

AUDLEY. (*Inquiringly.*) What! saved by him? 190

---

1   *windlass* Mechanism made up of a beam around which a rope or chain is wound, used
    for lifting a bucket from a well.

TALBOYS. When I fell there (*Pointing to well.*) half-stunned, yet eager for the safety of the woman who betrayed me, I crawled up the side, and seizing a desperate footing on the crumbling wall, I reached this spot, and hid myself in yonder thicket; he found me there that night.

AUDLEY. And you have been—

TALBOYS. Far, far away in other worlds; you'll hear the story from my lips ere long. I couldn't keep away. A voice within me dragged me back, a voice that cried out loudly to me to release her conscience from a double crime.

LADY A. (*Makes a movement towards Talboys as if entreating his compassion, he turns from her.*) He spurns me now! (*To Audley.*) And *you*—you have schemed and plotted to a noble purpose. You have your reward, Robert Audley. You have brought your victim to a living grave! (*After a look of fury at Audley, she lapses into a fixed stare, as of madness.*)

ALICE. (*Pointing to Lady Audley.*) See, see the look! the look that is in the picture!

LADY A. (*Pressing her head as if in pain—takes a step towards Audley, then stops, and throwing her arms up with a cry*) You have conquered a—MAD WOMAN! (*she sinks, supported by Alice and Phoebe.*)

ALICE. Dead!

AUDLEY. Not yet, not yet! The soul still lingers, but the mind, the mind is gone!

(*Curtain.*)

—1863

Differences between Braddon's Novel and Roberts's Play

George Roberts's adaptation, like other theatrical versions of *Lady Audley's Secret*, made the story far more streamlined than in Braddon's original examination of Lady Audley's unmasking. As Henry Morley suggested in his review of the play, the condensation of the three-volume novel into a two-act theater production resulted in a rushed, even antic, pace, with each shocking revelation rapidly followed by a no-less-shocking development.

The translation from page to stage also apparently necessitated the loss of some prominent characters. Most notably missing is Clara, George Talboys's sister, whom Robert Audley marries at the novel's conclusion; George Talboys then resides with the couple, ostensibly having sworn off marriage after the discovery of his wife's terrible duplicity. In the Roberts play, Robert Audley is instead pushed toward his cousin, renamed "Alice"—she is "Alicia" in the novel—though romance is hardly the focus of the drama. A number of critics have seen the play's omission of Clara as a tacit acknowledgment that heterosexual romance is little more than an incidental detail in Braddon's *Lady Audley's Secret*. It is rather, scholars of the sensation novel have suggested, the heterosocial romance between Robert Audley and George Talboys that animates the former's investigation into Lady Audley's past, and the joyous reunion of the two men when the latter is revealed to be alive that gives the work its happy ending.

In comparison with the novel, the play more insistently focuses on representing Lady Audley's crimes for maximum dramatic effect. Where the novel invests considerable time in the service of discovering Lady Audley's real secret—that her insanity is inherited from her mother, who was confined in an asylum—the play is devoted to staging an exaggerated version of her madness. Thus, while in the novel Lady Audley is given a long scene devoted to her family history, her childhood visit to her mother in the asylum, and her own experience of impassioned impulses, in the play, she merely proclaims herself a "MAD WOMAN" and collapses thereafter. And while the Lady Audley of Braddon's novel is sent to a Belgian asylum, Roberts's Lady Audley is nearly dead as the play concludes —though "[t]he soul still lingers ... the mind, the mind is gone!" What is more, in the play Sir Michael Audley dies before the revelation of his wife's crimes, but he is very much alive to receive her confession in the novel. Like Roberts, Braddon characterizes Lady Audley as the villain of the work, but the novel encourages interest in the psychological implications of her actions. In the hands of the male playwright, in contrast, Lady Audley is made an unambiguous monster, an inept, furious murderess fatally undone by her own duplicitous designs.

Though one should always be cautious in drawing direct biographical links, it seems not unreasonable to speculate in this case that Braddon's interest in madness and moral insanity may have been fed by the circumstances of those close to her; the first wife of Braddon's romantic partner—and eventual husband— John Maxwell was confined to a mental asylum. Certainly the story material of *Lady Audley's Secret* allowed Braddon to explore the subject of insanity and its effects on women—effects felt especially in the high rates of post-partum attacks of madness, known to the Victorians as puerperal insanity. These concerns are largely effaced in Roberts's play, which omits, for example, a lengthy consultation with a doctor that is included in the novel as part of the aftermath of Lady Audley's confession. The demands of the stage are of course different from the demands of the page, and Roberts's supple adaptation exploits the most immediately dramatic moments of the novel and represents second-hand descriptions for maximum effect.

The following passage is from Chapter 34 of the novel; it may be compared with the final scenes of Roberts's play.

from Mary Elizabeth Braddon, *Lady Audley's Secret* (1861–62)

... The woman [Lady Audley] rose suddenly and stood before him [Robert Audley] erect and resolute, with her hair dashed away from her face and her eyes glittering.

"Bring Sir Michael!" she cried; "bring him here, and I will confess anything—everything. What do I care? God knows I have struggled hard enough against you, and fought the battle patiently enough; but you have conquered, Mr. Robert Audley. It is a great triumph, is it not—a wonderful victory? You have used your cool, calculating, frigid, luminous intellect to a noble purpose. You have conquered—a MAD WOMAN!"

"A mad woman!" cried Mr. Audley.

"Yes, a mad woman. When you say that I killed George Talboys, you say the truth. When you say that I murdered him treacherously and foully, you lie. I killed him because I AM MAD! because my intellect is a little way upon the wrong side of that narrow boundary-line between sanity and insanity; because, when George Talboys goaded me, as you have goaded me, and reproached me, and threatened me, my mind, never properly balanced, utterly lost its balance, and *I was mad!* Bring Sir Michael; and bring him quickly. If he is to be told one thing let him be told everything; let him hear the secret of my life!"

Robert Audley left the room to look for his uncle. He went in search of that honoured kinsman with God knows how heavy a weight of anguish at his heart, for he knew he was about to shatter the day-dream of his uncle's life; and he knew that our dreams are none the less terrible to lose, because they have never been the realities for which we have mistaken them. But even in the midst of his sorrow for Sir Michael, he could not help wondering at my lady's last words— "the secret of my life." He remembered those lines in the letter written by Helen Talboys upon the eve of her flight from Wildernsea, which had so puzzled him. He remembered those appealing sentences— "You should forgive me, for you know *why* I have been so. You know the *secret* of my life."

He met Sir Michael in the hall. He made no attempt to prepare the way for the terrible revelation which the baronet was to hear. He only drew him into the fire-lit library, and there for the first time addressed him quietly thus: "Lady Audley has a confession to make to you, sir—a confession which I know will be a most cruel surprise, a most bitter grief. But it is necessary for your present honour, and for your future peace, that you should hear it. She has deceived you, I regret to say, most basely; but it is only right that you should hear from her own lips any excuses which she may have to offer for her wickedness. May God soften this blow for you!" sobbed the young man, suddenly breaking down; "I cannot!"

Sir Michael lifted his hand as if he would command his nephew to be silent, but that imperious hand dropped feeble and impotent at his side. He stood in the center of the fire-lit room rigid and immovable.

"Lucy!" he cried, in a voice whose anguish struck like a blow upon the jarred nerves of those who heard it, as the cry of a wounded animal pains the listener—"Lucy, tell me that this man is a madman! tell me so, my love, or I shall kill him!"

There was a sudden fury in his voice as he turned upon Robert, as if he could indeed have felled his wife's accuser to the earth with the strength of his uplifted arm.

But my lady fell upon her knees at his feet, interposing herself between the baronet and his nephew, who stood leaning on the back of an easy-chair, with his face hidden by his hand.

"He has told you the truth," said my lady, "and he is not mad! I have sent him for you that I may confess everything to you. I should be sorry for you if I could, for you have been very, very good to me, much better to me than I ever deserved; but I can't, I can't—I can feel nothing but my own misery. I told you long ago that I was selfish; I am selfish still—more selfish than ever in my misery. Happy, prosperous people may feel for others. I laugh at other people's sufferings; they seem so small compared to my own."

When first my lady had fallen on her knees, Sir Michael had attempted to raise her, and had remonstrated with her; but as she spoke he dropped into a chair close to the spot upon which she knelt, and with his hands clasped together, and with his head bent to catch every syllable of those horrible words, he listened as if his whole being had been resolved into that one sense of hearing.

"I must tell you the story of my life, in order to tell you why I have become the miserable wretch who has no better hope than to be allowed to run away and hide in some desolate corner of the earth. I must tell you the story of my life," repeated my lady, "but you need not fear that I shall dwell long upon it. It has not been so pleasant to me that I should wish to remember it. When I was a very little child I remember asking a question which it was natural enough that I should ask, God help me! I asked where my mother was. I had a faint remembrance of a face, like what my own is now, looking at me when I was very little better than a baby; but I had missed the face suddenly, and had never seen it since. They told me that mother was away. I was not happy, for the woman who had charge of me was a disagreeable woman and the place in which we lived was a lonely place, a village upon the Hampshire coast, about seven miles from Portsmouth. My father, who was in the navy, only came now and then to see me; and I was left almost entirely to the charge of this woman, who was irregularly paid, and who vented her rage upon me when my father was behindhand in remitting her money. So you see that at a very early age I found out what it was to be poor.

"Perhaps it was more from being discontented with my dreary life than from any wonderful impulse of affection, that I asked very often the same question about my mother. I always received the same answer—she was away. When I asked where, I was told that that was a secret. When I grew old enough to understand the meaning of the word death, I asked if my mother was dead, and I was told—'No, she was not dead; she was ill, and she was away.' I asked how long she had been ill, and I was told that she had been so some years, ever since I was a baby.

"At last the secret came out. I worried my foster-mother with the old question one day when the remittances had fallen very much in arrear, and her temper had been unusually tried. She flew into a passion, and told me that my mother was a mad woman, and that she was in a madhouse forty miles away. She had scarcely said this when she repented, and told me that it was not the truth, and that I was not to believe it, or to say that she had told me such a thing. I discovered afterward that my father had made her promise most solemnly never to tell me the secret of my mother's fate.

"I brooded horribly upon the thought of my mother's madness. It haunted me by day and night. I was always picturing to myself this mad woman pacing up and down some prison cell, in a hideous garment that bound her tortured limbs. I had exaggerated ideas of the horror of her situation. I had no knowledge of the different degrees of madness, and the image that haunted me was that of a distraught and violent creature, who would fall upon me and kill me if I came within her reach. This idea grew upon me until I used to awake in the dead of night, screaming aloud in an agony of terror, from a dream in which I had felt my mother's icy grasp upon my throat, and heard her ravings in my ear.

"When I was ten years old my father came to pay up the arrears due to my protectress, and to take me to school. He had left me in Hampshire longer than he had intended, from his inability to pay this money; so there again I felt the bitterness of poverty, and ran the risk of growing up an ignorant creature among coarse rustic children, because my father was poor."

My lady paused for a moment, but only to take breath, for she had spoken rapidly, as if eager to tell this hated story, and to have done with it. She was still on her knees, but Sir Michael made no effort to raise her.

He sat silent and immovable. What was this story that he was listening to? Whose was it, and to what was it to lead? It could not be his wife's; he had heard her simple account of her youth, and had believed it as he had believed in the Gospel. She had told him a very brief story of an early orphanage, and a long, quiet, colourless youth spent in the conventional seclusion of an English boarding-school.

"My father came at last, and I told him what I had discovered. He was very much affected when I spoke of my mother. He was not what the world generally calls a good man, but I learned afterward that he had loved his wife very dearly, and that he would have willingly sacrificed his life to her, and constituted himself her guardian, had he not been compelled to earn the daily bread of the mad woman and her child by the exercise of his profession. So here again I beheld what a bitter thing it is to be poor. My mother, who might have been tended by a devoted husband, was given over to the care of hired nurses.

"Before my father sent me to school at Torquay, he took me to see my mother. This visit served at least to dispel the idea which had so often terrified me. I saw no raving, straight-waist-coated maniac, guarded by zealous jailers, but a golden-haired, blue-eyed, girlish creature, who seemed as frivolous as a butterfly, and who skipped toward us with her yellow curls decorated with natural flowers, and saluted us with radiant smiles, and gay, ceaseless chatter.

"But she didn't know us. She would have spoken in the same manner to any stranger who had entered the gates of the garden about her prison-house. Her madness was an hereditary disease transmitted to her from her mother, who had died mad. She, my mother, had been, or had appeared sane up to the hour of my birth, but from that hour her intellect had decayed, and she had become what I saw her.

"I went away with the knowledge of this, and with the knowledge that the only inheritance I had to expect from my mother was—insanity!

"I went away with this knowledge in my mind, and with something more—a secret to keep. I was a child of ten years only, but I felt all the weight of that burden. I was to keep the secret of my mother's madness; for it was a secret that might affect me injuriously in after-life. I was to remember this.

"I did remember this; and it was, perhaps, this that made me selfish and heartless, for I suppose I am heartless. As I grew older I was told that I was pretty—beautiful—lovely—bewitching. I heard all these things at first indifferently, but by-and-by I listened to them greedily, and began to think that in spite of the secret of my life I might be more successful in the world's great lottery than my companions. I had learnt that which in some indefinite manner or other every school-girl learns sooner or later—I learned that my ultimate fate in life depended upon my marriage, and I concluded that if I was indeed prettier than my schoolfellows, I ought to marry better than any one of them.

"I left school before I was seventeen years of age, with this thought in my mind, and I went to live at the other extremity of England with my father, who had retired upon his half-pay, and had established himself at Wildernsea, with the idea that the place was cheap and select.

"The place was indeed select. I had not been there a month before I discovered that even the prettiest girl might wait a long time for a rich husband. I wish to hurry over this part of my life. I dare say I was very despicable. You and your nephew, Sir Michael, have been rich all your lives, and can very well afford to despise me; but I knew how far poverty can affect a life, and I looked forward with a sickening dread to a life so affected. At last the rich suitor, the wandering prince came."

She paused for a moment, and shuddered convulsively. It was impossible to see any of the changes in her countenance, for her face was obstinately bent toward the floor. Throughout her long confession she never lifted it; throughout her long confession her voice was never broken by a tear. What she had to tell she told in a cold, hard tone, very much the tone in which some criminal, dogged and sullen to the last, might have confessed to a jail chaplain.

"The wandering prince came," she repeated; "he was called George Talboys."

For the first time since his wife's confession had begun, Sir Michael Audley started. He began to understand it all now. A crowd of unheeded words and forgotten circumstances that had seemed too insignificant for remark or recollection, flashed back upon him as vividly as if they had been the leading incidents of his past life.

"Mr. George Talboys was a cornet[1] in a dragoon regiment. He was the only son of a rich country gentleman. He fell in love with me, and married me three months after my seventeenth birthday. I think I loved him as much as it was in my power to love anybody; not more than I have loved you, Sir Michael—not so much, for when you married me you elevated me to a position that he could never have given me."

The dream was broken. Sir Michael Audley remembered that summer's evening, nearly two years ago, when he had first declared his love for Mr. Dawson's governess; he remembered the sick, half-shuddering sensation of regret and disappointment that had come over him then, and he felt as if it had in some manner dimly foreshadowed the agony of to-night.

But I do not believe that even in his misery he felt that entire and unmitigated surprise, that utter revulsion of feeling that is felt when a good woman wanders away from herself and becomes the lost creature whom her husband is bound in honour to abjure. I do not believe that Sir Michael Audley had ever *really* believed in his wife. He had loved her and admired her; he had been bewitched by her beauty and bewildered by her charms; but that sense of something wanting, that vague feeling of loss and disappointment which had come upon him on the summer's night of his betrothal had been with him

---

1 *cornet* Standard-bearer in a cavalry regiment; an officer.

more or less distinctly ever since. I cannot believe that an honest man, however pure and single may be his mind, however simply trustful his nature, is ever really deceived by falsehood. There is beneath the voluntary confidence an involuntary distrust, not to be conquered by any effort of the will.

"We were married," my lady continued, "and I loved him very well, quite well enough to be happy with him as long as his money lasted, and while we were on the Continent, traveling in the best style and always staying at the best hotels. But when we came back to Wildernsea and lived with papa, and all the money was gone, and George grew gloomy and wretched, and was always thinking of his troubles, and appeared to neglect me, I was very unhappy, and it seemed as if this fine marriage had only given me a twelvemonth's gayety and extravagance after all. I begged George to appeal to his father, but he refused. I persuaded him to try and get employment, and he failed. My baby was born, and the crisis which had been fatal to my mother arose for me. I escaped, but I was more irritable perhaps after my recovery, less inclined to fight the hard battle of the world, more disposed to complain of poverty and neglect. I did complain one day, loudly and bitterly; I upbraided George Talboys for his cruelty in having allied a helpless girl to poverty and misery, and he flew into a passion with me and ran out of the house. When I awoke the next morning, I found a letter lying on the table by my bed, telling me that he was going to the antipodes to seek his fortune, and that he would never see me again until he was a rich man.

"I looked upon this as a desertion, and I resented it bitterly—resented it by hating the man who had left me with no protector but a weak, tipsy father, and with a child to support. I had to work hard for my living, and in every hour of labour—and what labour is more wearisome than the dull slavery of a governess?—I recognized a separate wrong done me by George Talboys. His father was rich, his sister was living in luxury and respectability, and I, his wife, and the mother of his son, was a slave allied to beggary and obscurity. People pitied me, and I hated them for their pity. I did not love the child, for he had been left a burden upon my hands. The hereditary taint that was in my blood had never until this time showed itself by any one sign or token; but at this time I became subject to fits of violence and despair. At this time I think my mind first lost its balance, and for the first time I crossed that invisible line which separates reason from madness. I have seen my father's eyes fixed upon me in horror and alarm. I have known him soothe me as only mad people and children are soothed, and I have chafed against his petty devices, I have resented even his indulgence.

"At last these fits of desperation resolved themselves into a desperate purpose. I determined to run away from this wretched home which my slavery supported. I determined to desert this father who had more fear of me than love for me. I determined to go to London and lose myself in that great chaos of humanity.

"I had seen an advertisement in the *Times* while I was at Wildernsea, and I presented myself to Mrs. Vincent, the advertiser, under a feigned name. She accepted me, waiving all questions as to my antecedents. You know the rest. I came here, and you made me an offer, the acceptance of which would lift me at once into the sphere to which my ambition had pointed ever since I was a school-girl, and heard for the first time that I was pretty.

"Three years had passed, and I had received no token of my husband's existence; for, I argued, that if he had returned to England, he would have succeeded in finding me under any name and in any place. I knew the energy of his character well enough to know this.

"I said 'I have a right to think that he is dead, or that he wishes me to believe him dead, and his shadow shall not stand between me and prosperity.' I said this, and I became your wife, Sir Michael, with every resolution to be as good a wife as it was in my nature to be. The common temptations that assail and shipwreck some women had no terror for me. I would have been your true and pure wife to the end of time, though I had been surrounded by a legion of tempters. The mad folly that the world calls love had never had any part in my madness, and here at least extremes met, and the vice of heartlessness became the virtue of constancy.

"I was very happy in the first triumph and grandeur of my new position, very grateful to the hand that had lifted me to it. In the sunshine of my own happiness I felt, for the first time in my life, for the miseries of others. I had been poor myself, and I was now rich, and could afford to pity and relieve the poverty of my neighbours. I took pleasure in acts of kindness and benevolence. I found out my father's address and sent him large sums of money, anonymously, for I did not wish him to discover what had become of me. I availed myself to the full of the privilege your generosity afforded me. I dispensed happiness on every side. I saw myself loved as well as admired, and I think I might have been a good woman for the rest of my life, if fate would have allowed me to be so.

"I believe that at this time my mind regained its just balance. I had watched myself very closely since leaving Wildernsea; I had held a check upon myself. I had often wondered while sitting in the surgeon's quiet family circle whether any suspicion of that invisible, hereditary taint had ever occurred to Mr. Dawson.

"Fate would not suffer me to be good. My destiny compelled me to be a wretch. Within a month of my marriage, I read in one of the Essex papers of the return of a certain Mr. Talboys, a fortunate gold-seeker, from Australia. The ship had sailed at the time I read the paragraph. What was to be done?

"I said just now that I knew the energy of George's character. I knew that the man who had gone to the antipodes and won a fortune for his wife would leave no stone unturned in his efforts to find her. It was hopeless to think of hiding myself from him.

"Unless he could be induced to believe that I was dead, he would never cease in his search for me.

"My brain was dazed as I thought of my peril. Again the balance trembled, again the invisible boundary was passed, again I was mad.

"I went down to Southampton and found my father, who was living there with my child. You remember how Mrs. Vincent's name was used as an excuse for this hurried journey, and how it was contrived I should go with no other escort than Phoebe Marks, whom I left at the hotel while I went to my father's house.

"I confided to my father the whole secret of my peril. He was not very much shocked at what I had done, for poverty had perhaps blunted his sense of honour and principle. He was not very much shocked, but he was frightened, and he promised to do all in his power to assist me in my horrible emergency.

"He had received a letter addressed to me at Wildernsea, by George, and forwarded from there to my father. This letter had been written within a few days of the sailing of the *Argus*, and it announced the probable date of the ship's arrival at Liverpool. This letter gave us, therefore, data upon which to act.

"We decided at once upon the first step. This was that on the date of the probable arrival of the *Argus*, or a few days later, an advertisement of my death should be inserted in the *Times*.

"But almost immediately after deciding upon this, we saw that there were fearful difficulties in the carrying out of such a simple plan. The date of the death, and the place in which I died, must be announced, as well as the death itself. George would immediately hurry to that place, however distant it might be, however comparatively inaccessible, and the shallow falsehood would be discovered.

"I knew enough of his sanguine temperament, his courage and determination, his readiness to hope against hope, to know that unless he saw the grave in which I was buried, and the register of my death, he would never believe that I was lost to him.

"My father was utterly dumfounded and helpless. He could only shed childish tears of despair and terror. He was of no use to me in this crisis.

"I was hopeless of any issue out of my difficulties. I began to think that I must trust to the chapter of accidents, and hope that among other obscure corners of the earth, Audley Court might be undreamt of by my husband.

"I sat with my father, drinking tea with him in his miserable hovel, and playing with the child, who was pleased with my dress and jewels, but quite unconscious that I was anything but a stranger to him. I had the boy in my arms, when a woman who attended him came to fetch him that she might make him more fit to be seen by the lady, as she said.

"I was anxious to know how the boy was treated, and I detained this woman in conversation with me while my father dozed over the tea-table.

"She was a pale-faced, sandy-haired woman of about five-and-forty and she seemed very glad to get the chance of talking to me as long as I pleased to allow her. She soon left off talking of the boy, however, to tell me of her own troubles. She was in very great trouble, she told me. Her eldest daughter had been obliged to leave her situation from ill-health; in fact, the doctor said the girl was in a decline; and it was a hard thing for a poor widow who had seen better days to have a sick daughter to support, as well as a family of young children.

"I let the woman run on for a long time in this manner, telling me the girl's ailments, and the girl's age, and the girl's doctor's stuff, and piety, and sufferings, and a great deal more. But I neither listened to her nor heeded her. I heard her, but only in a far-away manner, as I heard the traffic in the street, or the ripple of the stream at the bottom of it. What were this woman's troubles to me? I had miseries of my own, and worse miseries than her coarse nature could ever have to endure. These sort of people always had sick husbands or sick children, and expected to be helped in their illness by the rich. It was nothing out of the common. I was thinking this, and I was just going to dismiss the woman with a sovereign for her sick daughter, when an idea flashed upon me with such painful suddenness that it sent the blood surging up to my brain, and set my heart beating, as it only beats when I am mad.

"I asked the woman her name. She was a Mrs. Plowson, and she kept a small general shop, she said, and only ran in now and then to look after Georgey, and to see that the little maid-of-all-work took care of him. Her daughter's name was Matilda. I asked her several questions about this girl Matilda, and I ascertained that she was four-and-twenty, that she had always been consumptive, and that she was now, as the doctor said, going off in a rapid decline. He had declared that she could not last much more than a fortnight.

"It was in three weeks that the ship that carried George Talboys was expected to anchor in the Mersey.

"I need not dwell upon this business. I visited the sick girl. She was fair and slender. Her description, carelessly given, might tally nearly enough with my own, though she bore no shadow of resemblance to me, except in these two particulars. I was received by the girl as a rich lady who wished to do her a service. I bought the mother, who was poor and greedy, and who for a gift of money, more money than she had ever before received, consented to submit to anything I wished. Upon the second day after my introduction to this Mrs. Plowson, my father went over to Ventnor, and hired lodgings for his invalid daughter and her little boy. Early the next morning he carried over the dying girl and Georgey, who had been bribed to call her 'mamma.' She entered the house as Mrs. Talboys; she was attended by a Ventnor medical man as Mrs. Talboys; she died, and her death and burial were registered in that name.

"The advertisement was inserted in the *Times*, and upon the second day after its insertion George Talboys visited Ventnor, and ordered the tombstone which at this hour records the death of his wife, Helen Talboys."

Sir Michael Audley rose slowly, and with a stiff, constrained action, as if every physical sense had been benumbed by that one sense of misery.

"I cannot hear any more," he said, in a hoarse whisper; "if there is anything more to be told I cannot hear it. Robert, it is you who have brought about this discovery, as I understand. I want to know nothing more. Will you take upon yourself the duty of providing for the safety and comfort of this lady whom I have thought my wife? I need not ask you to remember in all you do, that I have loved her very dearly and truly. I cannot say farewell to her. I will not say it until I can think of her without bitterness—until I can pity her, as I now pray that God may pity her this night."

Sir Michael walked slowly from the room. He did not trust himself to look at that crouching figure. He did not wish to see the creature whom he had cherished. He went straight to his dressing-room, rung for his valet, and ordered him to pack a portmanteau, and make all necessary arrangements for accompanying his master by the last up-train.

Reviews of Mary Elizabeth Braddon's *Lady Audley's Secret*

The following reviews of Braddon's *Lady Audley's Secret* appeared in the Victorian press. Although most remark Braddon's talent as a writer, they consistently condemn her representation of a beautiful but deadly villainess and lament the public's appetite for sensation novels. The reviews also reveal the sum total of the novel's plot, including the disclosure of the eponymous "secret."

"Lady Audley's Secret," *The Times* (18 November 1862)

This review, published unsigned, was written by the Scottish journalist Eneas Swetland Dallas (1828–79).

The name of the novel which everybody is just now reading may excite the curiosity of historical students. They may imagine that it refers to that most horrible story which appears in the record of our State trials—the story of Mervyn Touchet, Lord Audley, who was beheaded in the reign of Charles I for inflicting on his wife, Lady Audley, indescribable cruelties. The secret of the imaginary Lady Audley, however, is very different, and the novel in which she figures belongs entirely to modern times. It's a good galloping novel, like a good gallop, to be enjoyed rather than criticized. It is full of rapid incident, well put together. When we begin to read we cannot choose but go on; and if, when we come to an end, we observe that we have travelled through a well-known country, that the ditches and hedges we have leaped are familiar to us, it is not to be supposed that in passing this criticism we are of necessity depreciating the work of a really clever authoress. The Greek dramatists wrote hundreds of plays, but the tragedians at least had only two stories to work upon. On the tale of Troy and the tale of Thebes[1] they rang innumerable changes, though with all that they had to relate their audiences were perfectly familiar. A modern

---

1   *tale of Troy* Cf. Homer's *Iliad*; *tale of Thebes* In Greek mythology and literature, Thebes is the location of several important stories, most notably Sophocles' Oedipus cycle, also known as the "Theban plays," and Euripides' *Bacchae*.

writer has to provide his readers with much greater novelties; the matter must be fresh and the treatment original; but if it is not entirely so, and if, in spite of that want, the writer succeeds in interesting the public, there is not much room for complaint. In plain English, the present writer has laid her hands upon some well-known materials,[1] but she has turned them to such good account, that in the general interest we forget the imperfections of detail, and in the rush of events take little note of what is new or what is hackneyed.

Miss Braddon's story belongs to a class of fiction which Mr. Wilkie Collins has rendered extremely popular, though he can scarcely be said to have invented it. Perhaps Edgar Poe[2] has done more than any other man to show the capacity of exciting imagination which this species of story affords. There is a secret, generally a crime, to be discovered. There are no apparent means of reaching the discovery. But our modern police regulations have gone far to reduce the detection of crime to a science, and there is nothing which the public are more eager to unravel than such mysteries as every now and then fill the newspapers. Suppose a carpet bag full of mangled remains found on Waterloo-bridge. That secret has never yet been penetrated, but once recognized as a secret, we know how the fascination of crime can be intensified by the fascination of mystery. Every little hint or clue is seized with astonishing avidity; countless suggestions are made and theories are started; millions of readers wait impatiently for more and more news; and the police and the newspaper offices are besieged by correspondents eager to propose new lines of inquiry. The secret which baffles the detectives, it is the province of the novelist to unravel. Whereas the old classical novel always had a villain to make all the mischief and the complications of the plot, and a hero to fight through those complications and to come off victorious by force of

---

1   *well-known materials* *Lady Audley's Secret* was thought by many Victorian readers to evoke aspects of the sensational case of Constance Kent, a sixteen-year-old who in the summer of 1860 was accused of murdering her four-year-old half-brother when his body—the throat slashed, chest stabbed—was discovered in an outhouse on the family's property. The case, which was not brought to trial until 1865, caused significant press excitement and attracted public attention, largely due to the persistent suspicion that the child had actually been murdered by his father Samuel Kent, who had been having an affair with the boy's nursemaid and killed the child after he discovered the elder Kent in a compromising position.
2   *Edgar Poe* Edgar Allan Poe (1809–49), American author best known for his dark tales incorporating psychological suspense and Gothic elements.

bravery or love or some irresistible sentiment; the modern fictions of which we speak delight chiefly in a villain and a villain-finder. The villain is the hero, and the villain-finder is set like a sleuth hound on his path. The fineness of scent which these animals display in fiction is amazing. Where to ordinary perception there is no appearance of anything wrong they detect in a word, in a look, far more than Lord Burleigh[1] ever intended. It is really delightful to see how the evidence accumulates bit by bit, and each bit in its proper place and at the proper time, in the most logical order. The acuteness of the villain-finder is preternatural. He sees a hand you cannot see, he hears a voice you cannot hear. At length, the final link in the chain of evidence is secure. In many cases the hunter has to go across the world for it—to Australia, to America, but he always finds it. The poor hunted beast is driven to bay; the secret is out, and the tale ends. Tell us not that the hunt is an old story, and that one hunt is like another. So it is; but whether over grass or over paper, it comes always new to the keen sportsman, and he who has been at the hunt oftenest enjoys it best. A foxhunter never seems to have enough of it, and a novel-reader will go on reading novels to all eternity, and sometimes even will have several in hand at once—a serial of Mr. Trollope's here, a serial of Mr. Dickens's there, and the last three-volume tale[2] into the bargain. To these readers we can promise abundance of excitement in the new story, which, indeed, is pitched in a key high enough to attract readers who usually care little for novels.

The most distinguished of the novelists who excite an interest in the analysis of evidence forbade the critics, when his last work appeared, to divulge his secret. To divulge it, however, could have done him no harm, and we do none to Miss Braddon when we say that the secret of Lady Audley is bigamy. We mention it the rather because it is characteristic of the modern novel. That the lady should be the centre of interest, that she should be the sinner of the tale, and that

---

1   *Lord Burleigh* William Cecil, 1st Baron Burghley (1521–98), adviser to Queen Elizabeth I. As a statesman, he is acknowledged by historians to have been especially adept at harnessing the power of literary works in public and political life.

2   *Trollope* Anthony Trollope (1815–82), Victorian novelist perhaps best known for his *Chronicles of Barsetshire*, a series of novels set in the fictional county; *Dickens* Charles Dickens (1812–70), perhaps the best known of Victorian writers; some of his novels featured sensational elements; *three-volume tale* Refers to the practice, common at this time, of publishing novels in three-volume editions.

her sin should be a violation of the marriage law are as natural to recent novels as that her guilt should be a secret, and a secret discovered by the most elaborate espionage. This is the age of lady novelists, and lady novelists naturally give the first place to the heroine. But, if the heroines have the first place, it will scarcely do to represent them as passive and quite angelic, or insipid—which heroines usually are. They have to be pictured as high-strung women, full of passion, purpose, and movement—very liable to error. Now, the most interesting side of a woman's character is her relation to the other sex, and the errors of women that are most interesting spring out of this relation. Hence unwonted prominence has of late been given to a theme which novelists used formerly to shrink from; and we are honoured with descriptions of the most hidden feelings of the fair sex which would have made our fathers and grandfathers stare. Truth to tell, however, the novelists have seldom been able to conjoin much analysis of feeling with much analysis of plot. If the novelist gets interested in the analysis of complications and the construction of evidence, he soon finds that he must ignore a good deal of passion, and do continual violence to character. On the other hand, if he works up character and elaborates sentiment, he finds to his cost that his story is being run away with. It is needful to keep the two apart, and we generally find female analysis in one class of novels, and the secret police system in another.

Without telling Miss Braddon's story, which is related with much skill, we may say that Lady Audley's character is well conceived, and develops itself naturally. In the first few chapters, she appears as a perfect angel, the beauty of the county, the delight of her husband, the beloved and admired of all who come within the reach of her spells. Gradually we discover a mask. She is a heartless creature who plays a heartless game. Her first husband sacrificed an excellent position in order to marry her, and she reproached him for the sacrifice. Adoring her with all his soul, he left her to recover himself in Australia. In his absence she flies from home, changes her name, obliterates all traces of her whereabouts, becomes a governess, as a governess wins the love of Sir Michael Audley, marries him, and is in the full enjoyment of wealth and position, when her husband returns. He returns to discover that she is dead. Nevertheless by means of those accidents which the novelists have always at command, he suddenly confronts her, and she deliberately murders him, or, at least, attempts to do so, and imagines that she has succeeded. It is not easy to represent a woman in such a position, or with a character capable of such acts; to combine so much beauty with so much deformity; to depict the lovely woman with the fishy extremities. Miss Braddon would be entitled to rank as the first of lady novelists if she had perfectly succeeded in reconciling these contradictions; nevertheless her portraiture is by no means feeble, and gives promise of great success hereafter. Some of the other characters, too, are well painted—that of Robert Audley, for example, who is here the villain-finder and the moral antithesis of Lady Audley. Whereas the latter is fair without and dark within, Robert Audley, her foe, is rough and uninviting without, but thoroughly good at heart. Indeed, it is seldom that one sees a novel so well balanced in the display of power, showing such *even* excellence of plot, of passion, of character, and of diction. This is the more remarkable, for, if report speak truly, Miss Braddon is the author of two or three novels, all appearing at the same time. So much facility is of itself a great gift; and much of the imperfection in the present novel it may be only fair to attribute to the strain upon the writer's pen. Hereafter, however, she can have no such defence. By means of her present work she acquires a position which ought to render impossible the extravagance of writing three novels at once.

Review of *Lady Audley's Secret, The Spectator* 1791 (1862)

The first edition of this story was sold, says the publishers, on the day of publication, and we could easily believe the fact, even had no Mr. Mudie[1] existed. Miss Braddon, whatever her true *status* in literature, at least "understands her epoch," and does not attempt to offer things too good for the public taste. She, like some much greater artists, has recognized the reviving taste for the horrible. People think themselves very enlightened now-a-days, and will not read about haughty barons and virtuous bandits, and haunted castles, and innocent victims flying from an unintelligible pursuit to an incomprehensible rescue.

---

1   *Mr. Mudie* Charles Edward Mudie (1818–90) established Mudie's Lending Library and Mudie's Subscription Library in 1842, with significant effects on Victorian publishing practices. His Library is often credited with contributing to the rise of the Victorian "triple-decker," or novel in three volumes.

But the old dish only wants new seasoning, and the classes who would once have read Mrs. Radcliffe now pore over stories as absurd as hers, but based upon criminal trials, Rosicrucian[1] theories, or the startling facts turned up by the students of morbid psychology. The old bandits are draped as French police, the Heroic Youth is a clever detective, and the Evil Being is generally a woman with a mysterious beauty, and still more mysterious capacity for meaningless wickedness. The author of *Lady Audley's Secret* has appreciated the popular taste, and constructed a story as wild in its incidents as any romance ever issued from the Minerva Press,[2] but modern in its machinery, and in the language in which that machinery is described. The stock Evil Being, who has committed a series of crimes, is a young lady of the period, with "flaxen hair, shot with gold," infantine ways, and a habit of making feeble sketches; the Innocent Victim is an Australian *emigré*, returned with plenty of nuggets, and the Avenger of Blood is a barrister, who hunts the Evil Being remorselessly, but talks humorous slang the while.

Sir Michael Audley, owner of Audley Court, has married in his old age a governess, of wonderful blonde beauty, who fascinates everybody with her gold hair and graceful childish ways, except her husband's nephew. He, a barrister of indolent temper and iron will, believes that she is a fiend guilty of the most monstrous crimes. He had a dear friend, just returned from Australia, whom he takes down to Audley Court, and who then disappears. A train of reflection, not very warrantable, convinces the barrister that his friend has been murdered, that his aunt was his friend's wife, and is now presumably his murderess; and he sets himself to discover her past history. The search occupies much of the book, is managed with the kind of skill which is so easy when one invents equally the key and the puzzle, and is at last successful. Lady Audley, after one ineffectual attempt to burn Mr. Audley alive, by setting fire to his inn, admits her guilt, and reveals the secret of her life. She is a mad woman, with the balance

---

1   *Mrs. Radcliffe* Anne Radcliffe (1764–1823), author of Gothic novels including *The Mysteries of Udolpho* and *The Romance of the Forest*; *Rosicrucian* I.e., esoteric, occult, philosophical. The Rosicrucians were a late-medieval society concerned with ancient truths about the natural world and the spiritual universe.

2   *Minerva Press* Publishing house well known for marketing Gothic fiction, especially by female authors, in the late eighteenth and early nineteenth centuries.

always trembling in her brain, and when it trembles a little too far she commits some great crime. At other times she is a yellow, infantine little woman, who bears sarcasm with a smile, and insolence with gentle deprecation, is always chilly, and exults intensely in the physical comforts around her won by her crimes. Mr. Audley, armed with his knowledge of her guilt, exposes her to her husband, and carries her off to Belgium, to be confined for life in a secluded madhouse. And then the missing husband turns up, the wife having only tried to murder him after all. That bare sketch really gives the substance of the novel, for beyond incident it contains nothing. There is a sub-love story scattered in bits about the book, but wholly devoid of interest, and for the rest, there is simply nothing. Most of the characters are lay figures. Mr. Audley might be one of "Waters'" detectives,[1] and the only character on which real pains have been bestowed is an artistic impossibility. We can imagine a tranquil criminal, but not a tranquil criminal who knows that two servants possess her secret, and that she herself, besides being a murderess, is a mad woman. Miss Braddon, moreover, fails throughout the story to give the slightest hint of this madness, which perhaps increases the surprise, but wholly destroys the artistic effect. Lady Audley leaves the impression, not of an evil woman, or a mad woman, or any definite kind of woman, but simply of a monstrosity,—a moral Julia Pastrana—a *lusus naturæ*,[2] whose aspect and movements excite only a dull and morbid curiosity. To justify the use of so exceptional a character, the author should have shown us her mind, painted the struggle with the momentary flashes of insanity, and the remorse which would so certainly have followed them; but she never lifts the veil. All we see of Lady Audley is what her gardener saw—a few acts and a great many little personal ways, throwing no light on her character beyond a suspicion that she has a vice extremely few women possess—physical selfishness. Of course, the laws of nature once set aside, it is easy to pile up horror. The sculptor who should make a figure with a woman's bust, and a beast's

---

1   *Waters' detectives* "Waters" was the pseudonym of the journalist William Russell, who published a series of real-life detective stories known as *Recollections of a Police-Officer* (1849–53).

2   *Julia Pastrana* Part of a European exhibition tour as the "Bearded and Hairy Lady," Pastrana (1834–60) was a Mexican woman who suffered from hypertrichosis, or excessive body hair, her face and body covered with black hair; *lusus naturæ* Latin: freak of nature.

head, and hoofed legs, and man's arms, would produce something striking enough; but he must not claim for his figure any place in the domain of true art. It is at best a bit of grotesquerie, and that is about the true value of *Lady Audley's Secret*. Of course it sells to a class, just as it pays somebody or other to advertise Julia Pastrana; for there are classes who love the horrible and the grotesque. We do not object particularly to their gratification—provided that those who cater to them are content with their true place in literature, which is not above the basement.

Review of *Lady Audley's Secret*, *The Critic* 25.631 (December 1862)

"Have you read 'Lady Audley's Secret?'" is now as frequent an inquiry as "Whether we had seen 'Lord Dundreary?'"[1] was three months ago. These popularities are strange facts to meditate upon; and to account for them would be next to impossible. The theatre-going English public has manifested intense delight in witnessing for more than a hundred nights, an English Lord represented, not even as a fool—but lower still—as an idiot; and now, the book before us, where the heroine is a murderess, a bigamist, and an incendiary, has run through five editions in as many weeks.

We pride ourselves upon being an aristocratic nation, and yet we laugh over, and thoroughly enjoy, the sad spectacle of Mr. Sothern's[2] impersonation of a British nobleman; we want ourselves over our Continental neighbours upon the superiority of the moral tendency of our light literature. Strange contradiction! those whom it is part of our political creed to uphold, the mass of the English people love to see degraded to the lowest specimens of humanity; and no sooner does a new novel issue from the press, where the principal character is a beautiful woman with an atrocious, devilish disposition, such as none among us ever met with, or few of us have dreamed of, than the book is anxiously sought after and greedily devoured. And when the idiot has been laughed at, and the three volumes closed, we ask "What the better men are we for either?" Has the spectacle been the means of

1   *Lord Dundreary* Character in Tom Taylor's play *Our American Cousin* (1858); Dundreary epitomizes the well-meaning but bumbling aristocrat.

2   *Mr. Sothern* Edward Askew Sothern (1826–81), English actor known for his portrayal of Lord Dundreary.

elevating our thoughts to what is true and noble in humanity? On the contrary, it has degraded them. Have we, by following the criminal course of a beautiful woman's life, gained one step in either our moral or intellectual progress? Far from it—we have retrograded. But this epidemic will surely be a fleeting one; we are made of better stuff and more healthy materials than to suffer under it long. The public taste, let us hope, will soon have a surfeit, and then resume its sounder tone. But the worst and most sad feature of its case is, that many of the best novelists of our day are pandering to feed these morbid tendencies— and for this reason we regret the more to see Miss Braddon joining their ranks and marching their course. For the authoress of "Lady Audley's Secret" is far from being a mediocre writer. This production of hers bears evidence to great ability, and talent of no mean order. The tale is eminently a fascinating one, despite its grave defects, and fascination is one of the greatest charms in works of fiction. German novel readers delight in a romance in which they are so deeply interested that they find it impossible to lay aside the book until they know the fate of the principal character concerned in it. And this is the case with "Lady Audley's Secret." Although we assure ourselves over and over again that no such creature as the heroine ever existed, that the whole fabric is an exaggeration and the events altogether impossible, still we are deeply interested in her fate; the hunting element within us is aroused, and we cannot rest until we know her end. Yet when it is over and we begin to consider the principal incidents round which the chief interest is centred, we remember that they cannot lay claim to originality. Lady Audley with her diabolical acts and golden curls, very strongly resembles Mr. Sala's Florence Armytage,[1] both in her charms and in her vices; the substitution of a dead for a living woman, and a false heading to a tombstone, recall to us forcibly an incident in Mr. Wilkie Collins's "Woman in White." Like the "Seven Sons of Mammon" and the "Woman in White," we have here incident upon incident related in the most easy and attractive manner; we have a complete series of what it is the fashion to call "sensation scenes," through which the reader's attention never flags. Pity it is that the authoress has not used her indisputable ability for novel writing

---

1   *Mr. Sala* George Augustus Sala, English journalist and author of the novel *The Seven Sons of Mammon* (1862); *Florence Armytage* In *The Seven Sons of Mammon*, Florence Armytage is a beautiful forger and blackmailer, who, at the end of the novel, dies in a French prison.

with a higher aim and a better purpose. The more we recongnise her gifts the more deeply do we deplore what we consider the misuse of it. But, while deploring it, we do not lose sight of the fact that, in pursuing the track which raised others to popularity, the temptation to do so was strong. The novel reading public has a keen relish just now for young and beautiful heroines who commit murders, forgeries, and all other atrocities. Enterprising publishers know this, and pay unprecedented sums for the wherewith to feed these morbid appetites; but if Miss Braddon's ambition leads her to hope for a more lasting fame, such as her talent fully entitles her to, we counsel her to walk upon a broader and safer road with steadier and less exaggerated steps.

The story she now gives to us is a strange, improbable one. A warm-hearted impulsive young guardsman marries the penniless daughter of a drunken naval lieutenant who had retired on half pay. This daughter is described as strangely beautiful, with soft blue eyes and "shimmering, feathery golden curls." Her fascinations were felt by every one she came in contact with, and "wherever she went she seemed to take joy and brightness with her." No wonder the young guardsman is captivated so quickly. But not so his father, who had never seen her. He refuses to have anything more to do with his son after his imprudent marriage; so the commission is sold, the money soon spent, and when the last shilling is neared, taunts and reproaches are heard from the beautiful lips of the young wife. In despair, George Talboys, the upbraided husband, rushes off to the gold fields of Australia, and in three years realises a handsome fortune. He returns full of love and joy and hope, only to read his wife's death in the *Times*, and to visit her grave in the quiet churchyard at Ventnor. But she is not dead, and soon the reader recognizes her in the brilliant Lady Audley—the wife of a rich old baronet, who dotes on her, and surrounds her with more than princely magnificence. George Talboys recognises her, too; circumstances bring them face to face, and she deliberately murders him—at least she intends to do so, for she throws him down a well in her own grounds. How little this foul deed troubles her light spirit may be seen from her behaviour on the same evening:

> Still my lady's pretty musical prattle ran on as merrily and continuously as the babble in some brook; and still Robert's thoughts wandered, in spite of himself, to George Talboys.

He thought of him hurrying down to Southampton by the mail train to see his boy. He thought of him as he had often seen him spelling over the shipping advertisements in the *Times*, looking for a vessel to take him back to Australia. Once he thought of him with a shudder, lying cold and stiff at the bottom of some shallow stream with his dead face turned toward the darkening sky.

Lady Audley noticed his abstraction, and asked him what he was thinking of.

"George Talboys," he answered abruptly.

She gave a little nervous shudder.

"Upon my word," she said, "you make me quite uncomfortable by the way in which you talk of Mr. Talboys. One would think that something extraordinary had happened to him."

"God forbid! But I cannot help feeling uneasy about him."

Later in the evening Sir Michael asked for some music, and my lady went to the piano. Robert Audley strolled after her to the instrument to turn over the leaves of her music; but she played from memory, and he was spared the trouble his gallantry would have imposed upon him.

He carried a pair of lighted candles to the piano, and arranged them conveniently for the pretty musician. She struck a few chords, and then wandered into a pensive sonata of Beethoven's. It was one of the many paradoxes in her character, that love of somber and melancholy melodies, so opposite to her gay nature.

Robert Audley lingered by her side, and as he had no occupation in turning over the leaves of her music, he amused himself by watching her jeweled, white hands gliding softly over the keys, with the lace sleeves dropping away from, her graceful, arched wrists. He looked at her pretty fingers one by one; this one glittering with a ruby heart; that encircled by an emerald serpent; and about them all a starry glitter of diamonds. From the fingers his eyes wandered to the rounded wrists: the broad, flat, gold bracelet upon her right wrist dropped over her hand, as she executed a rapid passage. She stopped abruptly to rearrange it; but before she could do so Robert Audley noticed a bruise upon her delicate skin.

"You have hurt your arm, Lady Audley!" he exclaimed.

She hastily replaced the bracelet.

"It is nothing," she said. "I am unfortunate in having a skin which the slightest touch bruises."

She went on playing, but Sir Michael came across the room to look into the matter of the bruise upon his wife's pretty wrist.

"What is it, Lucy?" he asked; "and how did it happen?"

"How foolish you all are to trouble yourselves about anything so absurd!" said Lady Audley, laughing. "I am rather absent in mind, and amused myself a few days ago by tying a piece of ribbon around my arm so tightly, that it left a bruise when I removed it."

"Hum!" thought Robert. "My lady tells little childish white lies; the bruise is of a more recent date than a few days ago; the skin has only just begun to change color."

Sir Michael took the slender wrist in his strong hand.

"Hold the candle, Robert," he said, "and let us look at this poor little arm."

It was not one bruise, but four slender, purple marks, such as might have been made by the four fingers of a powerful hand, that had grasped the delicate wrist a shade too roughly. A narrow ribbon, bound tightly, might have left some such marks, it is true, and my lady protested once more that, to the best of her recollection, that must have been how they were made.

Across one of the faint purple marks there was a darker tinge, as if a ring worn on one of those strong and cruel fingers had been ground into the tender flesh.

"I am sure my lady must tell white lies," thought Robert, "for I can't believe the story of the ribbon."

Robert Audley, the great friend of George Talboys, and nephew to Sir Michael Audley, suspects his beautiful childish aunt. Lazy man though he be, he traces out her antecedents, and in the end unmasks her, although she attempts to murder him also, by setting fire, in the dead of the night, to the inn where he is sleeping. She makes her own confession to her husband when she finds there is no possibility of escape from detection; but she remains a hardened beautiful sinner to the last. When her game was lost, and on the night of her confession, there is no change in her selfish sensuous nature. We read of her:

My lady slept. Through that long winter night she slept soundly. Criminals have often so slept their last sleep upon earth; and have been found in the gray morning slumbering peacefully, by the jailer who came to wake them.

The game had been played and lost. I do not think that my lady had thrown away a card, or missed the making of a trick which she might by any possibility have made; but her opponent's hand had been too powerful for her, and he had won.

She was more at peace now than she had ever been since that day—so soon after her second marriage—on which she had seen the announcement of the return of George Talboys from the gold-fields of Austr[al]ia. She might rest now, for they now knew the worst of her. There were no new discoveries to be made. She had flung the horrible burden of an almost unendurable secret off her shoulders, and her selfish sensuous nature resumed its mastery of her. She slept, peacefully nestled in her downy bed, under the soft mountain of silken coverlet, and in the sombre shade of the green velvet curtains. She had ordered her maid to sleep on a low couch in the same room, and she had also ordered that a lamp should be kept burning all night.

Not that I think she had any fear of shadowy visitations in the still hours of the night. She was too thoroughly selfish to care very much for anything that could not hurt her, and she had never heard of a ghost doing any actual and palpable harm. She had feared Robert Audley, but she feared him no longer. He had done his worst; she knew that he could do no more without bringing everlasting disgrace upon the name he venerated.

"They'll put me away somewhere, I suppose," my lady thought, "that is the worst they can do for me."

She looked upon herself as a species of state prisoner, who would have to be taken good care of. A second Iron Mask,[1] who must be provided for in some comfortable place of con-

---

1 *Iron Mask* The Man in the Iron Mask, a mysterious prisoner held by the French government during the seventeenth century. He wore a mask when transferred from one prison to another, and his identity was never revealed.

finement. She abandoned herself to a dull indifference. She had lived a hundred lives within the space of the last few days of her existence, and she had worn out her capacity for suffering—for a time at least.

She took a cup of strong green tea, and a few delicate fragments of toast the next morning with the same air of quiet relish common to condemned creatures who eat their last meal, while the gaolers look on to see that they do not bite fragments off the crockery, or swallow the teaspoon, or do any other violent act tending to the evasion of Mr. Jack Ketch.[1] She ate her breakfast, and took her morning bath, and emerged, with perfumed hair and in the most exquisitely careless of morning toilets, from her luxurious dressing-room. She looked round at all the costly appointments of the room with a yearning lingering gaze before she turned to leave it; but there was not one tender recollection in her mind of the man who had caused the furnishing of the chamber, and who in every precious toy that was scattered about in the reckless profusion of magnificence, had laid before her a mute evidence of his love. My lady was thinking how much the things had cost, and how painfully probable it was that the luxurious apartment would soon pass out of her possession.

She looked at herself in the cheval-glass before she left the room. A long night's rest had brought back the delicate rose-tints of her complexion, and the natural luster of her blue eyes. That unnatural light which had burned so fearfully the day before had gone, and my lady smiled triumphantly as she contemplated the reflection of her beauty. The days were gone in which her enemies could have branded her with white-hot irons, and burned away the loveliness which had done such mischief. Whatever they did to her they must leave her her beauty, she thought. At the worst, they were powerless to rob her of that.

The March day was bright and sunny, with a cheerless sunshine certainly. My lady wrapped herself in an Indian shawl; a shawl that had cost Sir Michael a hundred guineas. I think she had an idea that it would be well to wear this costly garment;

---

1   *Mr. Jack Ketch* Executioner; reference to a famously brutal executioner of the seventeenth century.

so that if hustled suddenly away, she might carry at least one of her possessions with her. Remember how much she had periled for a fine house and gorgeous furniture, for carriages and horses, jewels and laces; and do not wonder if she clings with a desperate tenacity to gauds and gew-gaws, in the hour of her despair. If she had been Judas, she would have held to her thirty pieces of silver to the last moment of her shameful life.

Her excuse for her conduct is that she is mad, that she inherits the taint of insanity from her mother, which fact, in truth, is Lady Audley's secret. In the end, her husband, George Talboys, turns up, although how he managed to get out of the deep well with a broken arm is a mystery which is not solved for the reader's benefit. This is, of course, but a brief, imperfect outline of the story. Let us hope, as we believe, that the heroine is an impossibility. But there are other characters in the book which are life-like, and are drawn admirably. Robert Audley, the indolent barrister, too indolent to hold a brief, shaking off his lethargic nature, learning that the game of life was not in his hands alone, rousing himself to energetic action through love for his friend; his is truly a masterly portrait. Here Miss Braddon shows that she possesses a clear insight into human nature; she causes him to possess conflicting and contrasting qualities, and makes life full of the inconsistencies which constitute a part of most of our daily lives. The scene, too, on the deck of the vessel, when George Talboys is returning home triumphantly with his hardly-earned gold, with not a cloud or doubt troubling his hopeful mind, or casting a shadow over the future. He pours forth his happy tale of love and success to a poor governess who had been in Australia for fifteen years, and was also homeward bound, to marry the man she has been engaged to through all that weary time. Much watching and waiting had brought distrust and doubt with them, and the poor governess looked not on the future so brightly and hopefully as did her joyous-hearted, trusting fellow-passenger. By degrees her doubting spirit steals subtly over his bright heart, and he becomes sad. It is but a sketch, but one that a master hand might be justly proud of. The book abounds in evidence of great talent; these, doubtless, make us hypercritical and jealous for future predictions.

Review of *Lady Audley's Secret*, *The Rose, the Shamrock and the Thistle* 2 (November 1862)

This unsigned review was presented under the heading "A Review of Books Written by or Addressed to Women."

The story over again of December loving May. Miss Braddon has long had a reputation which the incident and constructions of the present novel are likely to increase. From first to last the reader is well entertained, and her curiosity kept alive by the march of events. We are sorry the interest is principally derived from actions that all rightly constituted minds condemn; but whilst the novelist has to depict society, its wickedness cannot be passed over. If the faces are ugly, the true mirror must reflect their ugliness, however much the grace of virtue and simplicity be preferred. In the heroine we are introduced to an "old man's darling," who risks her position by a second marriage (her first husband being alive), which she hopes may be kept secret. Her husband, the baronet's invariable kindness and devotion, make this step all the more hateful and wicked; but the authoress in a measure palliates the delicate subject, by inferring that insanity is one of the afflictions common to Lady Audley's family. How in the end her secret is brought to light we leave readers to discover in Miss Braddon's own pages, and only add that sorrow follows in the footsteps of crime, and has to wash out with fresh tears every imprint left behind by passion in its sad wanderings—wanderings that we must term morbid and unreal, for we cannot call to memory a single instance in the history of devilry played by such a smiling fiend as the authoress portrays. It is the one great mistake of the book. A man may "smile, and smile, and be a villain;"[1] and so, indeed, under a smiling face a woman may conceal the cruellest hatred and all uncharitableness; but such a faired haired, child-like, petted, virtuous-seeming simpleton, never in nature carried a blight through the green landscape, as does Lady Audley through the novelist's pages.

---

1   *"A man … villain"* Cf. William Shakespeare, *Hamlet*: "one may smile, and smile, and be a villain; / At least I'm sure it may be so in Denmark" (1.5).

from "Our Female Sensation Novelists," *Christian Remembrancer* 46 (1863)

The following is excerpted from an unsigned review of the sensation novels of several female authors, including Caroline Norton, Ellen Wood, and Braddon, whose *Lady Audley's Secret* and *Aurora Floyd* are considered.

We have been counselled not to ask why the former times were better than these, and are thus instructed to beware of enhancing the past in peevish depreciation of the present, the scene of our labours and trials. The check is constantly needed by those whose past is long enough ago to melt into harmonious, golden, defect-concealing distance; but we are disposed to think that such check is never more required than when a comparison is forced upon us of the popular ideal of charming womanhood in the times we remember, and what seems to constitute the modern ideal of the same thing. This ideal may be gathered from the poetry, the romance, and the satire of both periods, as well as from closer experience. There was a time when the charge against young ladies was a morbid love of sermons and a too exclusive devotion to the persons that preached them; then they were the subjects of tender ridicule for a fantastic refinement; then they doted upon Fouqué and his Sintram,[1] and were prone to sacrifice solid advantages and worldly good things to a dream of romance; then it was interesting and an attraction, at least to seem to live in ignorance of evil; then they felt it good taste to shrink for publicity, and submitted to the rules of punctilio and decorum as if they liked them.... Those were the days before *Punch's*[2] generation of "fast young ladies" were born; while it would still have been a wild impossibility for the *Times* to announce beforehand that an Earl's daughter would, on such an occasion and in such a theatre, dance an Irish jig, and a still wilder impossibility for the lady to keep her engagement, and for the illustrated papers afterwards to represent the feat in the moment of execution.

---

1 *Fouqué* Friedrich Heinrich Karl de la Motte, Baron Fouqué (1777–1843), Romantic German author; *Sintram* Title character of *Sintram and His Companions* (1815), a much-admired novel by Fouqué.

2 *Punch Punch, or the London Charivari*, a popular English humor weekly founded in 1841.

We are not saying that the generation of which this is a feature is really a falling off from that other generation which furnishes us with such pleasant memories. Each has its developments for good or evil, sense or nonsense. The one is composed of the daughters of the other. The history of society is a series of reactions from faults it has become alive to. We know all this; but the popular literature of the day, which undertakes to represent the thought and impulses of its own time, almost forces us into a frame of disparaging comparison. The novels of twenty and thirty years ago, which told us a good deal we did not like of the society of the period, have passed into oblivion; the notions and tendencies of to-day find their exponents in novels in everybody's hands. They are peopled with characters which, if they go beyond our observation, and exceed anything we have seen, yet indicate plainly enough the direction manners have taken, and are accepted as a portrait of life by the general reader, through his very act of taking them into favour.

The "sensation novel" of our time, however extravagant and un-natural, yet is a sign of the times—the evidence of a certain turn of thought and action, of an impatience of old restraints, and a craving for some fundamental change in the working of society. We use the popular and very expressive term, and yet one much more easy to adopt than to define. Sensation writing is an appeal to the nerves rather than to the heart; but all exciting fiction works upon the nerves, and Shakspeare can make "every particular hair to stand on end" with anybody. We suppose that the true sensation novel feels the popular pulse with this view alone—considers any close fidelity to nature a slavish subservience injurious to effect, and willingly and designedly draws a picture of life which shall make reality insipid and the routine of ordinary existence intolerable to the imagination. To use *Punch's* definition in the prospectus of the *Sensation Times*, "It devotes itself to harrowing the mind, making the flesh creep, causing the hair to stand on end, giving shocks to the nervous system, destroying conventional moralities, and generally unfitting the public for the prosaic avoca-tions of life." And sensationalism does this by drugging thought and reason, and stimulating the attention through the lower and more animal instincts, rather than by a lively and quickened imagination; and especially by tampering with things evil, and infringing more or less on the confines of wrong. Crime is inseparable from the sensation novel, and so is sympathy with crime, however carefully the author professes, and may even suppose himself, to guard against this danger by periodical disclaimers and protests.

The one indispensable point in the sensation novel is, that it should contain something abnormal and unnatural; something that induces, in the simple idea, a sort of thrill.... All ghost-stories, of course, have the same feature. In one and all there is appeal to the imagination, through the active agency of the nerves, excited by the unnatural or supernatural. But the abnormal quality need not outrage physical laws; exceptional outrages of morality and custom may startle much in the same way. Bigamy, or the suspicion of bigamy, is sensational as fully, though in a lower field, as are ghosts and portents; it disturbs in the same way the reader's sense of the stability of things, and opens a new, untried vista of what may be. All crime that seems especially incongruous with the perpetrator's state and circumstances is of this nature, and offers a very ready and easy mode of exciting that surprise and sense of novelty which is the one indispensable necessity....

If Mrs. Norton attacks apparent and recognised respectability, professes to unmask false pretences, and shows that the worst people are those most in the world's good graces, Miss Braddon, the first and, at present, pre-eminent sensation writer, sets herself to defy and expose the real thing. Her bad people don't pretend only to be good: they *are* respectable; they really work, nay slave, in the performance of domestic duties and most accredited of all good works. The moral proper of her stories may be good or bad; as thus,—Lady Audley is wicked, and comes to a bad end; Aurora Floyd does a hundred bad things and prospers in spite of them, both in her own fate and in the reader's favour; but the real influence of everything this lady writes is to depreciate custom, and steady work of any kind whatever; every action, however creditable, that is not the immediate result of generous impulse. She disbelieves in systematic formal habitual goodness. She owns to a hatred of monotonous habit even in doing right. She declares for what she calls a Bohemian existence. She likes people to be influenced by anything rather than principle and cold duty; in fact, nerves, feeling, excitement, will, and inclination are the sole motive powers of every character she cares for. The person who goes on day after day doing stated duty-work because it is duty, not because she likes it, is a monster to her, a something hardly human. She regards such an one (that is, in her books) as a painful, oppressive phenom-enon. Not believing in the pleasures of habit of any sort, she can no more understand that there may be alleviations, hopes, nay positive joys, in a life of conscientious observances than could Timothy's Bess, in 'Adam Bede,' conceive it possible for life to have a single satisfac-tion to a person who wore such a cap as Dinah's.[1] The recoil from dul-ness is evidently too strong, and all regularity, all day by day uniform occupation is dull to her; and she has such a way of putting it that we confess there is a danger of its seeming dull to the reader also....

Three things seem to have aided in this war against steady unexcited well-doing, a familiarity at some time or the other with the drudgery of learning, and an equal familiarity with horses and with theatricals, not simply play-going, but life behind the scenes. Her heroines have all been disgusted by a routine education, some in their own person, some inflicting it on others.... The ordinary well-educated young lady, the flower and triumph of civilization, who has mastered her lessons, the languages, the history, the difficult passages in the sonata in C flat, and liked them all, is alternately an object of amusement and contempt....

It is in the existence of the real with the impossible that this writer's power lies.... People are apt to think, though it is no such thing, that the knowledge of ordinary custom-loving human nature is a much easier thing than knowledge of the waifs and strays of humanity, and this lady's experiences are ostentatiously of this exceptional kind. She would have us think that she views human nature generally in a scrape. Thus, she will ask, as if familiar with detectives and their mode of noting down their pencil memoranda, When they begin their pencils? and "how it is that they always seem to have arrived at the stump?" Again, one of her characters is intoxicated: "his head is laid upon the pillow, in one of those wretched positions which intoxication *always* chooses for its repose," as though she had seen so much of it. And it is with people in a scrape, or ready at any moment to fall into one, that she sympathises....

---

1 '*Adam Bede*' Novel by George Eliot (pseudonym of Mary Ann Evans), published in 1859. Bess is a character in the novel, as is Dinah Morris.

from H.L. Mansel, "Sensation Novels," *Quarterly Review* 113 (April 1863)

This unsigned review by Henry Longueville Mansel (1820–71), a respected Victorian philosopher and theologian, discusses several well-known sensation novels, including Braddon's *Lady Audley's Secret*, *Aurora Floyd*, Wilkie Collins's *No Name*, and Ellen Wood's *Danesbury House*.

... Not so the sensation novelist. No divine influence can be imagined as presiding over the birth of his work, beyond the market-law of demand and supply; no more immortality is dreamed of for it than for the fashions of the current season. A commercial atmosphere floats around works of this class, redolent of the manufactory and the shop. The public want novels, and novels must be made—so many yards of printed stuff, sensation-pattern, to be ready by the beginning of the season. And if the demands of the novel-reading public were to increase to the amount of a thousand per season, no difficulty would be found in producing a thousand works of the average merit. They rank with the verses of which "Lord Fanny spins a thousand such a day";[1] and spinning-machines of the Lord Fanny kind may be multiplied without limit.

Various causes have been at work to produce this phenomenon of our literature. Three principal ones may be named as having had a large share in it—periodicals, circulating libraries, and railway bookstalls. A periodical, from its very nature, must contain many articles of an ephemeral interest, and of the character of goods made to order. The material part of it is a fixed quantity, determined by rigid boundaries of space and time; and on this Procrustean bed the spiritual part must needs be stretched to fit. A given number of sheets of print, containing so many lines per sheet, must be produced weekly or monthly, and the diviner element must accommodate itself to these conditions. A periodical, moreover, belongs to the class of works which most men borrow and do not buy, and in which, therefore, they take only a

---

1   *"Lord Fanny ... a day"* Cf. Alexander Pope's *Imitations of Horace*. "Lord Fanny" is thought to be Pope's satirical representation of John Hervey, 2nd Baron Hervey (1696–1743), a courtier and memoirist. Hervey was rumored to be bisexual and to have carried on affairs with several men, and Pope presents him as a sexually ambiguous—and thus troubling—figure.

transitory interest. Few men will burden their shelves with a series of volumes which have no coherence in their parts, and no limit in their number, whose articles of personal interest may be as one halfpenny-worth of bread to an intolerable quantity of sack, and which have no other termination to their issue than the point at which they cease to be profitable. Under these circumstances, no small stimulus is given to the production of tales of the marketable stamp, which after appearing piecemeal in weekly or monthly installments, generally enter upon a second stage of their insect-life in the form of a handsome reprint under the auspices of the circulating library.

This last-named institution is the oldest offender of the three; but age has neither diminished the energy nor subdued the faults of its youth. It is more active now than at any former period of its existence, and its activity is much of the same kind as it was described in the pages of this Review more than fifty years ago. The manner of its action is indeed inseparable from the nature of the institution, varying only in the production of larger quantities to meet the demand of a more reading generation. From the days of the "Minerva Press" (that synonym for the dullest specimens of the light reading of our grandmothers) to those of the thousand and one tales of the current season, the circulating library has been the chief hot-bed for forcing a crop of writers without talent and readers without discrimination.... Subscription, as compared with purchase, produces no doubt a great increase in the quantity of books procurable, but with a corresponding deterioration in the quality. The buyer of books is generally careful to select what for his own purposes is worth buying; the subscriber is often content to take the good the gods provide him, glancing lazily down the library catalogue, and picking out some title which promises amusement or excitement....

The railway stall, like the circulating library, consists partly of books written expressly for its use, partly of reprints in a new phase of their existence—a phase internally that of the grub, with small print and cheap paper, externally that of the butterfly, with a tawdry cover, ornamented with a highly-coloured picture, hung out like a signboard, to give promise of the entertainment to be had within. The picture, like the book, is generally of the sensation kind, announcing some exciting scene to follow. A pale young lady in a white dress, with a dagger in her hand, evidently prepared for some desperate deed; or a couple of ruffians engaged in a deadly struggle; or a Red Indian in his war-paint; or, if the plot turns on smooth instead of violent villany, a priest persuading a dying man to sign a paper, or a disappointed heir burning a will; or a treacherous lover telling his flattering tale to some deluded maid or wife. The exigencies of railway travelling do not allow much time for examining the merits of a book before purchasing it; and keepers of bookstalls, as well as of refreshment-rooms, find an advantage in offering their customers something hot and strong, something that may catch the eye of the hurried passenger, and promise temporary excitement to relieve the dulness of a journey.

These circumstances of production naturally have their effect on the quality of the articles produced. Written to meet an ephemeral demand, aspiring only to an ephemeral existence, it is natural that they should have recourse to rapid and ephemeral methods of awakening the interest of their readers, striving to act as the dram or the dose, rather than as the solid food, because the effect is more immediately perceptible. And as the perpetual cravings of the dramdrinker or the valetudinarian for spirits or physic are hardly intelligible to the man of sound health and regular appetites, so, to one called from more wholesome studies to survey the wide field of sensational literature, it is difficult to realise the idea which its multifarious contents necessarily suggest, that these books must form the staple mental food of a very large class of readers....

The sensation novel, be it mere trash or something worse, is usually a tale of our own times. Proximity is, indeed, one great element of sensation. It is necessary to be near a mine to be blown up by its explosion; and a tale which aims at electrifying the nerves of the reader is never thoroughly effective unless the scene be laid in our own days and among the people we are in the habit of meeting. We read with little emotion, though it comes in the form of history, Livy's narrative of the secret poisonings carried on by nearly two hundred Roman ladies; we feel but a feeble interest in an authentic record of the crimes of a Borgia or a Brinvilliers;[1] but we are thrilled with horror, even in fiction, by the thought that such things may be going on around us

---

1 *Livy* Titus Livius Patavinus (59 BCE–17 CE), Roman historian; *Borgia* The Borgia family wielded a great deal of political and ecclesiastical power during the fifteenth and sixteenth centuries. Lucrezia Borgia (1480–1519), daughter of Pope Alexander VI, was rumored to have committed a series of crimes including incest and murder; *Brinvilliers* Marie-

and among us. The man who shook our hand with a hearty English grasp half an hour ago—the woman whose beauty and grace were the charm of last night, and whose gentle words sent us home better pleased with the world and with ourselves—how exciting to think that under these pleasing outsides may be concealed some demon in human shape, a Count Fosco[1] or a Lady Audley! He may have assumed all that heartiness to conceal some dark plot against our life or honour, or against the life or honour of one yet dearer: she may have left that gay scene to muffle herself in a thick veil and steal to a midnight meeting with some villanous accomplice. He may have a mysterious female, immured in a solitary tower or a private lunatic asylum, destined to come forth hereafter to menace the name and position of the excellent lady whom the world acknowledges as his wife: she may have a husband lying dead at the bottom of a well, and a fatherless child nobody knows where. All this is no doubt very exciting; but even excitement may be purchased too dearly; and we may be permitted to doubt whether the pleasure of a nervous shock is worth the cost of so much morbid anatomy if the picture is true, or so much slanderous misrepresentation if it be false....

Of particular offences, which are almost always contemporary and sometimes personal, undoubtedly the first place must be given to Bigamy. Indeed, so popular has this crime become, as to give rise to an entire sub-class in this branch of literature, which may be distinguished as that of Bigamy Novels. It is astonishing how many of our modern writers have selected this interesting breach of morality and law as the peg on which to hang a mystery and a dénouement. Of the tales on our list, no less than eight are bigamy stories:—"Lady Audley's Secret," "Aurora Floyd," "Clinton Maynyard," "Recommended to Mercy," "The Law of Divorce," "The Daily Governess," "Only a Woman," "The Woman of Spirit," all hang their narrative, wholly or in part, on bigamy in act, or bigamy in intention, on the existence or supposed existence of two wives to the same husband, or two husbands to the same wife.... The two first-named claim a notice as bigamy novels *par excellence*, the whole interest of the story turning on this circumstance. Though both exaggerated specimens of

---

Madeleine-Marguerite d'Aubray, Marquise de Brinvilliers (1630–76), French serial killer and inspiration for a number of fictional works.

1   *Count Fosco* Villain of *The Woman in White*.

the sensational type, they are the works of an author of real power, who is capable of better things than drawing highly-coloured portraits of beautiful fiends and fast young ladies burdened with superfluous husbands. Lady Audley, *alias* Mrs. George Talboys, is a Vittoria Corombona[1] transferred to the nineteenth century and to an English drawing-room. But the romantic wickedness of the "White Devil of Italy" suffers by being transplanted to home scenes and modern associations. The English White Devil, however, if not quite so romantic and interesting, is more than the rival of her prototype in boldness and guilt. She does with her own hand what Vittoria does by means of others. She has married a second husband, knowing or suspecting her first one to be still living; and the desperate means to which she has recourse to avoid discovery furnish an abundance of incidents of various degrees of ingenuity and villany. She advertises her own death in the newspapers, having previously procured a young woman who resembles her in person to die and be buried in her stead; she throws her first husband down a well, whence he finally emerges, we are not told how, with a broken arm; she breaks into a lawyer's chambers during his absence, and destroys his papers; she burns down a house to get rid of a dangerous witness, having locked the door of his room to prevent his escape. Yet, notwithstanding all the horrors of the story—and there are enough of them to furnish a full supper for a Macbeth—notwithstanding the glaring improbability of the incidents, the superhuman wickedness of the principal character and the incongruities of others; notwithstanding the transparent nature of the "secret" from the very beginning; the author has succeeded in constructing a narrative the interest of which is sustained to the end. The skill of the builder deserves to be employed on better materials.

---

1   *Vittoria Corombona* Main female character in John Webster's revenge tragedy *The White Devil* (1612), inspired by the 1585 murder of Vittoria Accoramboni, arranged by the powerful Medici family.

Reviews of George Roberts's *Lady Audley's Secret*

The following reviews of Roberts's adaptation appeared in the Victorian press. Like the reviews of the novel, these disclose the plot in its entirety. Note that because three adaptations of Braddon's novel appeared on London stages in 1863, some of the reviews inadvertently conflated and confused plot points from various dramatic versions.

"'Lady Audley' on the Stage," *The London Review* 6.140 (7 March 1863)

A new melodramatic play, the story of which is that of "Lady Audley's Secret," taken from the strange wild novel of Miss Braddon, whose sudden popularity is a significant literary phenomenon of the last few months, has this week been put upon the boards of the St. James Theatre. We have already expressed some dislike, on the grounds of morality and good taste, for this class of novels. These narratives of unredeemed depravity, while pandering to the morbid thirst for violent "sensation," can neither chasten, refine, nor invigorate the mind. They fail to perform that high function which was assigned by Aristotle to the tragic art when he said that its true use is "to purge the heart of man by pity and terror"; coming thus in aid of the solemn office of religion, with examples of a spiritual power surely avenging the perpetration of sin. Such, indeed, was the object of the earliest tragedians, whose works have been preserved to us from that heroic age of Greece, when, at Athens, the old soldier of Marathon wielded his poetic "thunder-phrase"[1] to enforce the inviolability of the moral law, by depicting, in the Furies of conscience, the fearful messengers of the gods. And such, too, was the aim of our own Shakespeare, faithful to the same idea, which reason had suggested to the heathen, and which Christianity has more certainly revealed,—that the visitations of re-

---

1   *old soldier of Marathon* Aeschylus, ancient Greek writer of tragedies;   *"thunder-phrase"* Cf. Robert Browning, *Sordello* (1840): "The thunder-phrase of the Athenian, grown / Up out of the memories of Marathon."

morse are sent into the presence of the guilty mind by a judicial infliction, and emanate from the sphere of supernatural power. The tent of Richard, the banquet-hall of Macbeth, haunted by the ghosts of their slain, bear witness, along with the fatality brooding in the atmosphere of their final acts and preparing their foreseen destruction, to this awful lesson of a Divine punishment of crime, in the appointed anguish of the soul which has sinned. That weird imagery, however, of the medieval or classical mythologists will not do for modern fiction. Unless the now fashionable tales of adultery and murder are to display the wreck of human nature within the breast, as an effect of violating the laws imposed by the sovereign will and wisdom ruling all, they will not serve for the moral instruction of this age. It may, however, be allowed, that a story is not always bound to supply express moral edification. To enlarge the range of our sympathies, by interesting us in the joys and sorrows, the hopes and fears, of its various personages, and by calling upon us to share the conflict of good and evil motives which divide their hearts, is still more properly its aim.

But it is essential that they should be characters with whom we *can* sympathize—that they should be capable of good, though struggling with evil, and perhaps overcome by it—that they should be human beings, and not mere demoniac impersonations of unrelenting vice. We cannot feel any real interest in the mental sufferings which may be conventionally attributed to such a one as Lady Audley, since we never find her touched by any generous or tender affection. We can understand her dread of detection and vengeance, but not her remorse. A compound of the coarsest worldly ambition, with fiendish malignity and pride, though tricked out in the external graces of womanhood, has about her so little that is feminine, or even that is human, as to make it difficult to conceive her feelings, unless she were physically tortured, or hanged. It might be possible to feel for other persons of the story, or even to feel with them, but that they are thoroughly commonplace. Mr. Robert Audley, for instance, is the ordinary type of social detective, who, like Mr. Walter Hartright in "The Woman in White," is obliged, by his private acquaintance with the victim of a mysterious villany, to undertake the task of its exposure. And his friend, her ladyship's first husband, whether dead or alive, behaves in so inconsequential a manner, that, while we think no man was ever more badly used, we cannot heartily echo Robert

Audley's vow, "Heaven help those who stand between me and the secret, for they shall all be sacrificed to the memory of George Talboys!" The fact is, that all the characters in the book, and all the readers of it, are, "Heaven help them!" sacrificed to "the secret," which, after the middle of the first volume, is no secret at all.

Being, therefore, neither a story with a moral purpose nor one truly illustrative of human character, nor one fitted to exercise the affections and sympathies with an innocent and natural play of feeling, this novel has yet proved attractive to many readers. And so, the reports of the trial of Constance or Catherine Wilson[1] may have seemed attractive to them as a narrative of extreme and almost incredible wickedness; over which they linger, detained by that sort of fascination which a sight of some monstrosities in nature has been said to exert. It is, perhaps, the more attractive to those once brought within its sway, because it seems so repulsive to those who view it from a distance, still walking on "on maiden meditation, fancy free."[2] At first view, the notion that a very pretty, ladylike young woman, decorated with a waxen complexion, blue eyes, and golden hair, will compass the death of several men for the sake of maintaining her position as the wife of a country baronet, gives rather a disagreeable shock to our sense of social security and to our habitual esteem for the lovelier sex. But this rare specimen of feline craft and cruelty, as she is safely caged with the covers of Miss Braddon's three volumes, affords a piquant gratification to those who more closely study her caressing gambols, without any fear of her claws. Indeed, we are even disposed to believe that, if the lady existed in real life, and, having escaped the sentence of the criminal law, were eligible in the matrimonial market, she might, after a month's publicity in the police-courts and assize-courts, receive as many proposals from suitors for her hand as were made notoriously to a renowned female poisoner at Edinburgh, after her acquittal, three or four years ago. Supposing the motive which had prompted her crimes to be past, the vanity of her new possessor might be tickled with the idea of caressing so perilous a creature.

Lady Audley, as she appears this week upon the stage, is the same person that we found her three or four months since, in a deplor-

---

1   *Catherine Wilson* British serial poisoner, hanged in 1862.
2   *"on maiden ... fancy free"* Cf. Shakespeare, *A Midsummer Night's Dream* (2.1)

ably successful book. If the public recognition if Miss Braddon's undoubted cleverness as a writer must be qualified with sincere regret, that an Englishwoman should have chosen for her literary model the abnormal creations of Balzac, we have no scruple in giving to Miss Herbert, as an actress, the praise of having thoroughly entered into the spirit of her part with an intellectual grasp of its utmost capabilities, which even improves upon the author's conception. If she has much rant to utter, it is no fault of hers. Nor is she ill-supported by the other performers, slight as is the interest of their parts. That of Luke Marks, the debauched, dishonest, grumbling gamekeeper, by whose agency, rather than by Robert Audley's ingenious pursuit, her ladyship's crimes are discovered, is played by Mr. Frank Matthews, the manager, with a humorous appreciation of the roughest manners of rustic low life; while Mr. Arthur Stirling, in the part of Robert Audley, and Mr. Gaston Murray, as the unfortunate Talboys, do their obvious business in a vigorous and manly style. The scenery, expressly painted for this play by Mr. Beverley from the laboured descriptions in the novel, has more than one good pictorial effect. Of the drama itself, as compressing within two hurried acts the leading events and dialogues of a story but too familiar to most readers of the popular fictions of the day, it is needless that we should say much. It will, however, be readily understood, that the unnatural behaviour and the improbable incidents, upon which the forced complications of "Lady Audley's Secret" depend, do not become less glaringly offensive, when detached from the less salient passages of the book and placed in close sequence upon the stage. The actual meeting of Talboys with his unfaithful wife, the altercation between them, and their mutual threats and defiance just before she throws him down into the well, serve only, as they are introduced into this play, to show yet more than in the novel how absurd is the notion that any woman in that position, though it were to save herself from an accusation of bigamy, would at once resort to open and deadly violence, instead of trying, by hypocrisy and blandishments, to disarm the anger of a man who passionately loved her. And though, in the duel of sharp insinuations and evasions which afterwards takes place between Robert Audley and the suspected murderess, the skill of both performers is most effectively displayed, we are struck with the fact that Lady Audley never attempts to seduce the man whom she has so much cause to fear, and so, while affecting to share his anxiety, stifle his first suspicion by the influence of her natural attractions. She prefers to burn him to death in his bed. In this respect, at least, the story is free from one objectionable element—that of the illicit love. It has nevertheless, in our judgment, an unwholesome moral tendency. It is an appeal to the low taste for criminal horrors which is sufficiently catered for by the Old Bailey[1] reports, without enlisting the arts of the novelist or the dramatist for its prurient gratification. We cannot approve its success.

"St. James's Theatre," *The Rose, the Shamrock and the Thistle* 2 (April 1863)

This unsigned review, though highly complimentary, makes a glaring error in its presentation of the play's plot by conflating the Roberts version with William Suter's adaptation. Lady Audley "escapes [the] doom" of the lunatic asylum by consuming poison in the very dramatic conclusion of Suter's play; the Roberts adaptation instead concludes with Lady Audley's collapse as she is overcome by her madness.

St James's Theatre.—"Lady Audley's Secret," produced; adapted by Mr. George Roberts, with consent of the authoress, from Miss Braddon's popular novel. If we make no mistake in our prediction, Miss Herbert of the St James's theatre will be, in the future, as much identified with the character of *Lady Audley* as Mr. Sothern at the Haymarket is identified as the veritable *Dundreary*. The success of this piece is real and sudden, and this is as it should be, for the stage has rarely, if ever, been adorned by finer scene-painting, and by more striking acting in the case of the principal part, or by careful persona-tion of the secondary parts. It was Miss Herbert's good fortune to be at once accepted by the audience, as exactly suited in personal appearance to personate the fair-haired, brilliant and fascinating blonde, *Lady Audley*; but far higher merit is displayed by the *actress* in giving a vitality to the intriguing, daring and accomplished hero-ine of Miss Braddon's novel,—indeed, Miss Herbert not only *looked*

---

1   *Old Bailey* Central Criminal Court in London; accounts of the trials held there were issued regularly.

Lady Audley, but really was that *titled* sinner, such as she lives in the book, and those who have read the work will know what subtlety, undaunted courage and double-faced dissimulation must be portrayed before a likeness to the original could be produced. That such a likeness *is* produced, is Miss Herbert's last and greatest triumph. The drama exhausts in two acts the plot of the novel. *George Talboys* finds himself compelled to leave his wife and seek a fortune in Australia. Returning to England he reads an account of his wife's death. Meanwhile, his wife has re-married to *Sir Michael Audley*, a baronet with a grown-up daughter, and the kind old man is completely under the influence of his young and second wife. The latter's present position is next threatened by a visit to Audley Court by *Robert Audley*, the baronet's nephew, who brings with him his friend—and by a fatality this friend is *Talboys*, the first husband. A recognition takes place in the library: the lady recriminates her husband's reproaches; he had abandoned, deserted her, and now must leave her in peace. He threatens to expose her. Then comes the first grand outburst of passion! *Lady Audley* dares him to do it. "Do it—at your peril," she exclaims, springing before him like a fury. A struggle ensues, during which an opportunity occurs in the grounds, and *Lady Audley* takes the fatal moment, to thrust her husband off his balance into a well. Does remorse follow? not a pang, but a feeling of exultation, and the wretched woman bounds back into the library, ringing out the one word, "free." But the end is not yet; *Robert Audley* seeks to account for his friend's sudden disappearance and, watching his uncle's young wife, makes him suspect her; and he loses no opportunities of thrusting home hints and questions; these are all parried with excellent skill, and this duel of words in polite life, is one of the most finished performances ever witnessed on the stage. *Lady Audley*, however, sees that *Robert* suspects, perhaps knows, her secret, and she continues to be offended with the visitor to Audley Court, and *Sir Michael* inhospitably shows his nephew the door. The guest goes to the village inn, where lives *Luke Marks*, now the landlord, but formerly the under-gamekeeper to *Sir Michael*. This *Marks* had witnessed the scene between *Lady Audley* and her first husband, and had afterwards rescued the drowning man from the well, and, as a means to extort money from his former mistress, *Marks* keeps *Talboys* concealed. The climax is then brought about by the wretched woman visiting the inn the very night that *Robert Audley* takes refuge there. She has been again summoned under a new threat of exposure, and whilst she is pacifying the drunken landlord, *Robert* overhears the conversation, and he feels he has now sufficient grounds to expose the murderess of his friend. The chance of doing is scarcely allowed him, for *Lady Audley* contrives to set fire to the old house, and escapes to the *Lime Tree Avenue* leading up to Audley Court. Whilst here remorse fastens on her heart for a time: in the sighing of the wind she hears moaning voices, the voices of the dead: then the moon-lighted walk becomes ruddy, the house is now on fire, and courage comes again to *Lady Audley* as she thinks both the men, who are masters of her secret, are perishing in the burning ruin. At this time the turret bell tolls at Audley Court; the baronet has suddenly died, whilst a group of servants and villagers come round, attracted by the house on fire, from which, half-dressed, *Robert Audley* is seen escaping. He seeks the lady, and at once denounces her as a murderess. Of course she scorns his words; then *Luke Marks*, nearly burnt to death, is brought on a litter to make his dying confession to "Master Robert," and, at this moment, the excitement of the audience is at its highest pitch. Still, against all statements, the lady displays indomitable courage, and demands proof! Whilst the very words are on her lips, the husband she believes to be drowned re-appears, and the guilty woman is overwhelmed at last: then when threatened with the lunatic asylum, which the insanity of her crimes shows to be her proper home, she escapes that doom by taking poison, and this ends the drama. The acting of Mr. Frank Matthews, Mr. Arthur Stirling, and of Mr. Gaston Murray, in rather weak parts, was highly finished and careful, and the two set scenes of the *Library* and *Lime Tree Walk* are, in themselves, the most satisfactory of any we have seen anywhere.

from "The Theatres," *Musical World* **41.11 (14 March 1863)**

> This unsigned review considers *Lady Audley's Secret* alongside several other productions, including a theatrical adaptation of Braddon's *Aurora Floyd* then being performed on London stages.

The drama founded on *Lady Audley's Secret*—at the St. James's Theatre—will disappoint admirers of Miss Braddon. It does not follow that because a novel is good a play founded upon it must be also good. Frequent attempts have been made to dramatize *Tom Jones*,[1] and with one uniform result—failure. The plan of a story and the treatment of its characters may be too homely for a play. On the other hand, unmitigated atrocity, which in narrative loses half its horrors, may be difficult to render endurable on the stage—at any rate, on the English stage, and in modern drama. Lady Audley is a sort of mild Lucrezia Borgia, with scarcely her provocations, and without her years and experience. The success of the new play we cannot but think almost exclusively due to Miss Herbert's "buskin"[2] and Mr. W. Beverley's "brush." Miss Herbert (Lady Audley) surprised by her tragic face; Mr. Beverley surprised nobody by the beauty of his pictures. They are, however, worthy of each other. *Lady Audley's Secret* is given nightly, and draws large audiences.

---

1   *Tom Jones* *The History of Tom Jones, a Foundling* (1749), a popular comic novel by Henry Fielding.
2   *"buskin"* I.e., dramatic style.

from the publisher

A name never says it all, but the word "broadview" expresses a good deal of the philosophy behind our company. We are open to a broad range of academic approaches and political viewpoints. We pay attention to the broad impact book publishing and book printing has in the wider world; we began using recycled stock more than a decade ago, and for some years now we have used 100% recycled paper for most titles. As a Canadian-based company we naturally publish a number of titles with a Canadian emphasis, but our publishing program overall is internationally oriented and broad-ranging. Our individual titles often appeal to a broad readership too; many are of interest as much to general readers as to academics and students.

Founded in 1985, Broadview remains a fully independent company owned by its shareholders—not an imprint or subsidiary of a larger multinational.

If you would like to find out more about Broadview and about the books we publish, please visit us at **www.broadviewpress.com**. And if you'd like to place an order through the site, we'd like to show our appreciation by extending a special discount to you: by entering the code below you will receive a 20% discount on purchases made through the Broadview website.

Discount code: **broadview20%**

Thank you for choosing Broadview.

Please note: this offer applies only to sales of
bound books within the United States or Canada.

LIST
of products used:

269 lb(s) of Rolland Enviro100 Print
100% post-consumer

Generated by : www.cascades.com/calculator

Sources : Environmental Paper Network (EPN)
www.papercalculator.org

RESULTS
Based on the Cascades products you selected
compared to products in the industry made with
100% virgin fiber, your savings are:

 2 trees

 2,225 gal. US of water
24 days of water consumption

 281 lbs of waste
3 waste containers

 731 lbs CO2
1,387 miles driven

 4 MMBTU
17,343 60W light bulbs for one hour

 2 lbs NOX
emissions of one truck during 3 days

RECYCLED
Paper made from
recycled material
FSC® C103567